HOW TO RETIRE YOUNG & RICH

THE EDITORS OF MONEY

CONTENTS

INTRODUCTION

YOUNG PEOPLE PLANNING THEIR RETIREMENT? Twenty- and thirty-watzits plotting out their pensions? At first the idea sounds morbid. A bit like designing your headstone. But poll after opinion poll in recent years has come up with the same conclusion: saving enough for retirement has become one of the two or three top preoccupations among American adults of all ages.

Just think about it for a minute and it makes perfect sense. Retirement used to be that last brief stage of life. Social Security and a small pension would see most people through it just fine. Now look at retirement: 30 years, maybe half of them in robust health—maybe all of them the way medical science is advancing.

What we have before us is nothing less than a second chance at life, the opportunity to start all over again, older of course, but wiser and not a lot worse for wear. Early retirement, you say? Show that to your grandparents and they'd see it for what it really is: two lives instead of one. But not, alas, two lives for the *price* of one. And there's the rub. People are leaving their jobs earlier and living longer. And they know instinctively, even those fresh from college, that it's going to take a heap of cash to get you through your second lifetime. Thus the issue becomes both a lasting joy and an early sorrow. It's wonderful to know that life will be healthy and long. But the polls also reveal that most people fear they will never be able to accumulate enough to retire early *and* to pay for it all.

And they're right. Most of them won't have enough saved up by the time they're ready to call it quits. And many will take the leap anyway, only to go broke halfway through their golden years. But you? Will you be one of the clever minority who succeed in retiring young and rich enough to live comfortably well into your 90s?

First here's the answer you expect: Read this book and you'll find out how to do it. The younger you are, the better your chance of retiring young and rich. But even if you are within a few years of retirement, you should not give up. Just as retirement has spread out to encompass three decades, young and rich have altered their meanings as well. If you are able to retire at 45, say, you may have four decades or more to look forward to. By any standard, that's young. And the new definition of rich is even simpler to grasp: having enough to see you through to the end of a long, active life.

To get there from here, four concepts have to get hammered deep into your psyche so that you will see the challenge with such blinding clarity that you will be radicalized and will ACT. These four ideas are not new; you know them well. What you may not realize is that they undergird all of the strategies that will be unfolding later on in this book. That's why they are taking a bow right here:

INFLATION: The unstoppable tide that washes away your savings. Next to plain stupidity, inflation is nature's greatest impediment in building a superior nestegg and keeping it from running out. Always must be taken into account as you plan ahead.

GROWTH INVESTMENTS: The ones that do best over time and the only ones that consistently beat inflation. Primarily stocks and stock mutual funds.

COMPOUND INTEREST: Alias the miracle of compounding. The marvelous mushrooming effect created by the interest you earn on principal plus the interest you earned earlier on that same principal, and so on. Income that compounds on a tax-deferred basis is the best. For instance, $10,000 compounding at a rate of 8% a year inside a tax-deferred IRA would grow to $21,600 in 10 years, $46,600 in 20 years and $100,627 in 30 years.

ALONENESS. Also known as You're On Your Own. The daddy and mommy who used to do it all for us, tucking us comfily into our later years, have both run out of money and, if truth be told, out of concern for us. Those financial parents are Uncle Sam, with his Social Security benefits; and our employer, who used to put all the money we needed into our pensions and just hand them over to us at retirement. Uncle Sam now sees Social Security as an entitlement, and an entitlement is something that has to be cut. If you're young now, write off at least half of what your parents are expecting (or getting) from Social Security. And those traditional pensions have turned into monstrous money-eaters. They're being replaced by new-fangled pensions called 401(k)s and such. But they don't pay you as much as the old ones did. And besides, who stays around a company long enough to build up a real penson anyway? So now you really need that 401(k). But you also need to save and invest on your own. Once you had two caring money parents. Now you're a semi-orphan. But you've got a plan. And here it is...

So it is just good common sense and prudent insurance of future security for today's employees to have an escape hatch from a career that is about to be cut off. Since this is not a book about careers, just be aware that there are dozens of other books that tackle the great contemporary issue of job security. If you haven't already plotted out your escape from job death, search out one or more of these books and don't rest until you have figured out how to keep your income high and assured until you retire.

CHAPTER 1

WHAT YOU NEED TO DO NOW

TO RETIRE YOUNG AND RICH. If you could see it, it would probably be a beach. If you could smell it, it would be rum, limes and suntan lotion. If you could hear it, what else? The surf. This fantasy may be the most shopworn cliche of all—the eternal vacation. But it symbolizes one of the deepest of human yearnings—freedom. What it doesn't do is get you closer to the reality. In fact, the fantasy can turn into an opiate, unless you figure out the way to turn the dream into a well focused goal. And to do that you will have to rearrange some of the furniture in your life. For example, you almost certainly will need to figure out a way to spend less so you can save more. Sounds like a drag, and undoubtedly it will be uncomfortable at first. But it's that old unavoidable: reality. And yes, you ought to do it soon. Now is best.

This chapter is about the handful of things that you should do as soon as possible. They will serve as the foundation of your dream. In time they will turn it into a plan with a built-in safety net. So take these four strategies to heart as seriously as though you were signing a contract for life. Indeed, to work, that's what they have to be.

1. LEARN TO SAVE MORE THAN YOU EVER DREAMED YOU COULD.

Here's why this rule is the most basic of all. As stated in the Introduction to this book, the savers and investors of this world are now largely on their own. Social Security and pensions together will not be enough to carry you through your longer life. You will need to open your retirement drive on a third front—your own savings.

And as you will see when you figure out how much you will need to retire in Chapter 3, your own savings may need to be substantial to cover a long post-work period. For instance, let's say your household income at retirement is $80,000 a year. You even wait until you're 65 to call it quits. Financial planners use a rule of thumb that people on average will need 80% of their pre-retirement income to maintain the same living standard later on. And say you estimate you will live 20 more years and that the inflation rate will average 4% a year over that time. How much will you need? A cool $1.17 million. If you figure to live 30 more years—and many planners say it's wise to make that assumption to be sure your money doesn't run out before you do—you will need $2.18 million.

That's the demand side of the picture. You will need lots of money for your long later life. Very challenging. Now let's take a look at the supply side: you. Also very challenging, because of the widespead belief among middle-class Americans that trying to save is futile. It's hard all right, but it isn't futile. Here's why:

We live in a hyper-consumer economy. More than economy, really: it's a consumer culture, bred in the bone and impossible to escape unless you quit society entirely and live alone in the desert. This culture knows not the face of self-denial. It has forgotten the concept of postponed pleasures upon which middle-class life was built. So you must accept the proposition that you are deeply affected by this culture, that you are really part of it. Then you must realize that when someone says, "I just can't save a cent," that person really believes what he or she is saying. Then you must learn to resist a kneejerk agreement and a supportive "That's right!" Instead, at least to yourself, you must substitute a skeptical "Let's look at the record."

For starters, saving is far from easy. But two powerful forces are at work to make the problem seem unsolvable—perception and superficial reality. The perception is the sense of powerlessness fueled by the strongest desire to consume ever known to humankind; the reality is the higher cost of everything we consume, starting with housing and education.

Yet ask any expert on credit or financial planning and you'll be told that the bottom-line reality is something quite different: unless you are truly poor, there is always some "give" in your budget, something that can be cut far short of the bone. One frivolous image comes to mind: all the young folk who consume several $3 *caffe lattes* each day while complaining that they'll never be able to afford to buy a home of their own. Should they deny themselves the pleasure of good coffee? Not necessarily. It's just that today's superconsumers have holes in their jeans they don't even know are there. What they have surely never done is to figure out how much those holes are costing them, how much a home would cost them, comparing the two sides of the ledger and then making an informed decision about what really matters to them most.

So if retiring young and rich appeals to you, or even if you're more motivated by not retiring old and poor, you will have to save regularly. And the amount you'll have to save will probably be a lot more than you now save or think you can manage. You'll see how much when you get to Chapter 3. For the time being, let's follow the consensus advice of financial experts who say that from your 30s on—that is, once you get settled in your career with expectations of regular raises as well as increasing expenses—you should be aiming at saving at least 10% of your pre-tax income. You make $50,000 a year? If you're not saving at least $5,000 of that, you're falling behind. And you know what that means: If you start saving in earnest sometime later on, you may have to hike that percentage to 20% or more to make up not only for the savings you didn't stash, but for the investment returns you didn't get along the way.

Here, then, without undue tedium or slogging, are the basics on how to save regularly:

First of all, take a Saturday afternoon and sit down with your checkbook and a record of your credit-card charges for the past 12 months. Segregate all your bills by cagetory for the last 12 months. Then tot up each category. So at the end you will see how many dollars you spent over the past year on housing, utilities, eating out, travel, clothing and so on. Unless you are an unusually astute bookkeeper, the results should surprise you—some of the results, that is. You will begin to get a sense of just where you have been overspending and, thereby, just where you will be able to cut back in order to beef up your savings.

To help you zero in on the culprit categories, here is a general estimate of the ideal range for each. There are two sets here—one for young singles in their 20s and one for couples in their 40s with two incomes and two children.

	SINGLES	COUPLES WITH TWO KIDS
Housing	20-25%	30%
Loan payments	13-15	13-15
Food	10-15	10-15
Child care	0	8-10
Entertainment	7-14	3-7
Vacations	3-7	3-7
Pocket money	8-12	5-8
Transportation	7-10	7-10
Clothing, personal care	4-8	4-10
Education	5-7	5-7
Utilities	4-7	4-7
Contributions	2-7	2-5
Savings	5-10	10
Insurance	1-3	3-5

You should also try to make as much of your savings as possible automatic. That way there won't be any of those poignant struggles with yourself over the tragedy of self-denial. If it doesn't go through your hands, you won't miss it. At least you won't miss it the way you would if you had to part with it painfully every month. Your first automatic savings vehicle should be your company savings plan, because of the tax savings and, often, the matching dollars tossed in by your employer. (More on that later below.) Many corporations also make regular payroll deductions and put the proceeds into a bank account or mutual fund for you. Or automatic transfers can be made from your checking account each month to your mutual fund company.

You can also use the "pay yourself first" approach. You simply make sure that your retirement savings are among the first of the bills that you pay each month. This may require an enormous change in the way you or your spouse think about saving. For instance, many financially sophisticated people nevertheless believe that the only way to handle their accounts is to pay down all of their debts before saving anything. So long as you have credit card obligations outstanding, for instance, nothing goes for retirement.

This is a grievous error in thinking because it robs you of those twin dynamos that make your savings grow so amazingly—growth stocks and compound interest. For example, if you set out to save $1 million by the time you were 65, assuming an average annual return of 7%, here's how dramatically your contributions and the actual earnings of your savings would vary depending on when you begin. If you start saving at 35 and therefore have 30 years to save, you will have to put $820 a month into your account. At the end of the 30 years, your contributions will amount to $300,000; the other $700,000 will come from the investment earnings. But if you start at 60, with only five years to save, you will have to put in $13,870 a month and $840,000 of your own hard-earned, after-tax dollars; only $16,000 will come from investment return.

Another technique is to commit your next raise to savings. The easiest way to to this, of course, is to call your company payroll department and have the raise put into your employee savings plan. You can also promise yourself that any windfalls that come your way—from a tax refund to a spot bonus to an inheritance—will go into your savings.

2. MAX OUT ON YOUR 401(K) OR OTHER TAX-DEFERRED RETIREMENT PLAN.

If you're making headway with Strategy Number 1, Number 2 will be easy. That's because you will be saving enough to be able to put the maximum amount of dollars into your tax-deferred plan. If you work at a company that offers a 401(k) plan to employees, grab it. This should be where your first savings dollars go. Only when you have put as much as possible into your 401(k) should you then go on to other ways to invest. What else not only defers taxes while your money is working but does it on a before-tax basis?

Yet even that isn't what really makes 401(k)s so central to getting richer younger. The twin pistons powering these savings vehicles are taxes, taxes, taxes; and compounding, compounding, compounding. Together, tax deferral and compounding make dollars multiply as nothing else can do. Here is an astounding illustration: Take a 35-year-old who earns $60,000 a year and puts 6% of his salary into a taxable investment that earns 8% a year. By age 65, he would have accumulated a total of $185,744 after paying taxes at a rate of 30%. By contrast, if he were to take that same amount of money and put it into a tax-deferred account like a 401(k) or IRA, his pile would have grow to more than double the taxed amount—to a lofty $407,820 when he reached 65.

You can improve even on that if your employer matched your 401(k) contribution, as most do. Typical match is 50 cents on the dollar, up to a certain percentage of salary, usually 6%. The employee can usually put in up to 10% of his or her salary up to a limit of more than $9,000.

Other tax-advantaged plans that may be appropriate for you:

- Traditional deductible IRAs: You get to deduct from your income tax contributions of up to $2,000 per person per year in an IRA. But if you are already enrolled in a company plan, you can fully deduct your IRA contribution only if you earn less than $30,000 (for singles) or $50,000 (for married couples filing jointly). (These threshholds are for tax year 1998 and rise annually thereafter.) If you and your spouse are part of no company plan, you can take the full deduction. So generally,IRAs are best for those who have no company plans.
- Roth IRAs.These are the newer, streamlined version of IRAs and may be even more advantageous than the traditional type, particularly for younger people. (Check with your accountant or financial planner.) Each spouse of a married couple with a total adjusted gross income of as much as $150,000 ($95,000 for singles) can make a $2,000 contribution each year to a Roth IRA, even if he or she has a retirement plan at work. You pay taxes on the contribution, which builds up tax-free. After you're 59 1/2, you can take all your money out tax-free.
- 403(b)s: These are similar to 401(k)s but for employees of schools and charitable organizations.
- Keoghs. These are terrific ways for small business owners funding plans for themselves and their employees to stash big hunks of income in tax-deferred accounts. They're complicated and sophisticated, so anyone ready to take one on may need help from an accountant.
- Annuities. These come in two varieties, variable and fixed. They're best for people who have put the maximum into other tax-deferred plans.

3. NEVER ENDANGER YOUR PRINCIPAL.

In other words, be an investment realist, neither too risk-prone nor too risk-averse. To retire young and rich, even if you start saving in your

20s, even if you put most of your money in growth stocks, even if you max out on your tax-favored plans at work—in short, even if you follow all the textbook do's and don't's, you may still not accumulate enough savings in time if you aren't clear on the issue of risk. What it comes down to is simple: you will want to sensitize yourself gradually to almost instictively taking the right amount of risk. Then your investments will grow fast, but not so fast that they burn out.

All this sounds ludicrously obvious. In theory, that is true. But in practice, many investors become obsessed with fear, put all their money into 5% bank CDs and watch from behind their triple-locked doors as their returns over the years are entirely consumed by inflation.

On the other hand, many other investors are enflamed by greed, often whipped to this frenzy by even greedier stockbrokers who get them to put their money into superrisky investments that flame out and leave nothing behind. This path is far more damaging than the meek and fearful route. At least there you are left with your principal. But when you lose big, you have to win double-big to make up. In fact, one of the first things investment pros learn is that if you lose 50% your money, you have to make up 100% just to break even. Getting into that predicament either makes you give up and retreat to the safety of CDs, or redouble your risk and set yourself up for a greater fall the next time.

The sensitizing process mentioned above is especially delicate for people at either extreme of the risk spectrum: too timorous or too daring. As you absorb Chapter 5, How to Invest in Your Future, you'll see this need for balancing risk take on concrete form.

4. PUT A SAFETY NET UNDER YOUR EARNING CAPACITY.

The last foundation factor that is absolutely essential to achieving your goal is your steadily improving income. This also may seem resoundingly obvious. But in today's economy it is far from it. Hundreds of thousands of professionals and manager in their 40s and 50s have been let go by downsizing companies in recent years. Their stories are by now familiar to any newspaper or magazine reader or TV news watcher. These people by and large walked out into a completely different job climate from the one that prevailed when they last were looking for work. After years of trying, many of them had to face the bitter reality that they would never again be employed at the same high rate of pay. Many had to settle for far lesser jobs. And many more entered a kind of enforced early retirement. For such people, retirement planning and saving stopped dead the day their downsizing companies let them go. Their future looks bleak as they slowly but surely run out of money.

So it is just good common sense and prudent insurance of future security for today's employees to have an escape hatch from a career that is about to be cut off. Since this is not a book about careers, just be aware that there are dozens of other books that tackle the great contemporary issue of job security. If you haven't already plotted out your escape from job death, search out one or more of these books and don't rest until you have figured out how to keep your income high and assured until you retire.

CHAPTER 2

WHAT TO DO ABOUT SOCIAL SECURITY

IT'S BECOME UNQUESTIONED DOGMA among experts on personal finance that your retirement fund, to be adequate, must draw on three main sources: your company plans, your own individual savings and investments, and Social Security. The problem with this scenario is that hardly anybody believes it.

Just look at a recent national study of affluent baby boomers, pre-retirees and retirees by Equitable Life. All three groups agreed that their company plans are their single most important retirement income source: 48% of boomers, 43% of pre-retirees and 40% of retirees voted for company plans. Next came individual investments, which got the nod from 18% of boomers, 23% of pre-retirees and 15% of retirees. What about Social Security? It landed in last place generally. But its showing was so low as to be ignominious: only 2% of boomers, 3% of pre-retirees and 14% of retirees voted Social Security their single most important income source.

True, these are affluent people: the median income of the boomers in the survey is $84,000 a year and $93,000 for the pre-retirees. But their biases are typical and you'll find them expressed in any recent poll on the subject. The most famous instance is the survey revealing that more adults under the age of 34 believe in UFOs than think they'll get any Social Security at all. It is practically a given in boomer thinking that by the time they get there, Social Security won't be around to take care of them. And with the first boomers destined to turn 55 in 2001, and presumably start their early exodus from the workforce around then, it won't be very long before we see if their gloomy outlook is correct.

Well, is it? Emphatically, no. Social Security will continue to be an important element of retirement income for most Americans as far as the eye can see into the next century. Right now, in fact, it is far more generous a contributor to retirement finances than most people realize. For instance, the maximum benefit available to a 65-year-old is more than $16,000 a year. If that person's spouse was the same age and also entitled to the maximum benefit—a pretty typical case in a two-professional household—the couple would be receiving more than $32,000 a year, partially tax-free, from that source alone. They would have needed an investment portfolio worth $400,000 to produce that much income, assuming a return of 8%.

If that doesn't impress you, the cost-of-living (COLA) factor might. Unlike your pension, which almost always stays petrified at the same amount for as long as you live, your Social Security benefit rises with inflation. And at 3% a year, any benefit would double in around 24 years.

Because Social Security is such an emotional and political issue, it is useful to stop a minute and look at where we are:

Unless Congress does a 180-degree turnaround, Social Security will remain a supersensitive political issue that no politician would dare take on. But everyone knows that something has to be done about Social Security before it wrecks the federal budget. The Social Security trust fund is slated to begin running deficits in 2013. That's when the first boomers turn 67. Between 2010 and 2030, the army of Social Security beneficiaries will grow by about a half, adding 26 million more people to the rolls. But the number of workers supporting the system will stay just about flat, a perfect recipe for disaster.

The best guess available is that Congress will somehow not be stupid enough to allow this mountainous problem to grow too big before doing something about it. Then benefits would take draconian cuts and disaster would have arrived. So look for fixes to be applied sometime within the next decade. They will consist of a combination of: 1) increased taxes on benefits (today as much as 85% of benefits may be taxed, depending on your income; 2) further raising of the retirement age (it's scheduled to begin moving up from 65 to 67 in the year 2003); and 3) lowering of the cost-of-living allowance, which lately has been adding between 2% and 3% or so a year to checks.

The crucial point is that none of these moves, alone or in combination, will destroy Social Security as we know it. Much of the sense of coming doom has been issuing from two sources, both of which are studded with conflicts of interst. The first is politicians of both major parties, who have made a practice of charging that their opponents are scheming to cut Social Security benefits. Often the accusations have no substance. No wonder Social Security has been called the third-rail of politics: touch it and you die.

The second source of confusion is financial planners (for more on planners, see Chapter 8). If a planner can project little or no income from Social Security for a client, that means that the client has to save and invest more to make up for the shortfall. And that helps a planner's case if he or she is earning fat commissions by selling you annuities, mutual funds or other financial products.

So let's get serious about what you can look forward to, and how to ensure you get what you're entitled to.

The first thing to do is to get a formal readout of your work history and projected benefits from the Social Security Administration. All you have to do is to call the SSA at 800-772-1213 and ask for a projection of your annual benefit. A few weeks later, you'll get a detailed report stating the approximate size of your benefit-to-be, based on your income history and an estimate of how much you'll make between the present and your retirement. If you're 55 or older, in fact, you already should have begun to get an automatic annual report of your benefit projections from the SSA.

Getting this accounting is important for two reasons: first, you will be better able to correct any errors of omission the SSA might have made on your record. While such mistakes are not common, the chances of their occurring have increased with the accelerated job-hopping that has become part of our work culture. Second, you will be able to figure out how much you need (coming up in the next chapter) much more accurately.

HOW YOUR AGE MATTERS

Age has its privileges, an old rule that has new meaning when it comes to Social Security benefits. The older you are, the better off you are. The rundown starting with those who will be the most affected:

Born in 1960 or later. You'll get the biggest hit. The generations who have enjoyed Social Security benefits from the outset in 1935 have by and large taken out of the system far more than they put in. For you, it will be the reverse. A worker who retired in 1980, by one estimate, received $63,000 more in Social Security benefits than he put in (calculated in 1985 dollars). You, on the other hand, will likely be allowed to keep only half of your projected benefit. On top of that, those born in 1960 or later will face a normal retirement age of 67 instead of 65; and early retirement at 62, which brings 80% of full benefit today, will bring only 70%.

Born between 1938 and 1959. You'll feel some pain, but not a serious amount. For instance, those born in 1950 will see their normal retirement age rise to 66, from today's 65. The figure increases slightly each year until the year 2027, when it hits 67 years for those born in 1960. And early retirement at age 62 will bring you 75% of your full Social Security benefit, down from 80% now.

Born before 1938. Your benefits are safe and you won't have to deal with any of the pushing back of the normal retirement age. You should expect, however, to feel an increasing tax burden on your benefit check. Currently 50% of your benefits are taxed when your "provisional" income (that's adjusted gross income plus tax-exempt interest and half of your Social Security benefits) exceeds $35,000 on a joint return ($25,000 for a single). And when your provisional income runs over $44,000 on a joint return ($34,000 if you're single), then up to 85% of your benefit is subject to federal income tax. You should expect that this trend toward taxing more and more of your Social Security benefit will continue. It would be wise to expect that if your retirement income is more than $50,000 or $60,000 a year, you'll pay income tax on most if not all of your Social Security.

WHEN YOU SHOULD START

If you retire early, you can choose when to start taking your Social Security benefits. As you now know, waiting gets you more and waiting longer gets you even more. Sometimes it's wise to wait, sometimes it isn't. A rundown of your options:

Start at 62. This means you'll spend the rest of your life collecting only 80% of what you might have gotten had you just waited three years. But on the other hand, it will take a long time even at a full benefit to make up for the three years of checks you might have been collecting. Perhaps the best way to decide is to look at how you will be financing the early years of your retirement. If giving up those Social Security checks between 62 and 65 means drawing on your investments, then you are probably better off taking the checks right away and leaving your portfolio intact, particularly if it's in growth investments with potential for big returns.

Start at 65. If you have other sources of income that make it unnecessary to draw on your investments, then it would be a good idea to put off Social Security until 65. Also, if you think you will be re-entering the job market from time to time, as many early retirees do, that would be a strong reason for putting off your Social Security checks. Under 65, you lose $1 of Social Security benefits for every $2 of earned income above $8,160. If you're between 65 and 69, the bite is reduced slightly to $1 of benefits for every $3 you earn above $11,280.

Start at 70. This can mean a big difference in your check because it goes up a bit for every single month you delay starting past age 65. Lately the amount has been an additional 4.5% a year, but it nearly doubles to 8% in the year 2008 and thereafter. That would increase a monthly check by more than 25% over the normal retire-at-65 rate. You should think about delaying until 70 if you plan to have earned income during much of your 60s despite retirement, or if you come from a long-lived family. Remember also that the higher your benefit the higher your spouse's survivor benefit after you die. Which brings up our last Social Security discussion:

HOW YOU QUALIFY

You can become eligible for Social Security benefits in one of five ways:

1) With your own benefits, based on your lifetime work record;
2) With spousal benefits, based on your husband's or wife's work record (normally half of the spouse's full benefit);
3) With divorced spouse's benefit (providing you were married at least 10 years, your former spouse is receiving Social Security or is more than 62 years old, you are not remarried and you have been divorced for at least two years);
4) With widow's or widower's benefits (providing you were married at least nine months and did not remarry before you turned 60); or
5) With divorced widow's or widower's benefits (providing you were married to your ex-husband or ex-wife at least 10 years, are 60 or older and married your present spouse before age 60).

CHAPTER 3

THE KEY: HOW MUCH YOU WILL NEED

WHATEVER AGE YOU ARE, if you haven't figured out how much you need to save, now is the time to do so. If you're close to retirement, it's vital you find out now to determine how ready you are to stop receiving a paycheck. On the other hand, let's say you are in your early 20s, just starting out, making a modest entry-level wage, single and totally enthusiastic about 1) retiring early; and 2) an Armani suit, a Mazda Miata and two weeks in the Greek islands. By knowing the tradeoffs, you are much likelier to go for 1) and forego most or all of 2). And the simple facts are these: If you are 35 years from retirement, by starting now and saving 10% of your income each year, you can expect to accumulate enough by the end of your career to retire. That's assuming you get a 9% annual gain on your money and inflation runs 3% a year.) But if you wait just 10 more years, and start saving when you are 25 years away from leaving work, you'll have to put away something like 21% of your pay.

Don't try using the above rule of thumb to figure your own needs, though. It's too rough and the individual variables can change the numbers substantially. Instead, take a few minutes to fill out at least one of the two worksheets we provide in this chapter. .

To make your job as simple as possible, in fact, you can skip the first worksheet—WHAT YOU'LL SPEND WHEN YOU RETIRE—if you like. This is where you get to estimate what percentage of your pre-retirement income you will need to live on after you stop working. It's a worthwhile exercise because younger retirees almost always spend considerably more than older, less mobile ones. Besides, the younger ones vary widely in their spending, from roughly 50% of pre-retirement pay for those who stay close to home and putter in the garden to 120% for those who live out the travel adventures they have been dreaming of for a lifetime. If you decide to leave this worksheet blank, however, just use the rule of thumb many planners employ: you'll need 80% of your pre-retirement pay in retirement.

WHAT YOU'LL SPEND WHEN YOU RETIRE

This, as we noted above, is optional but highly recommended. In the "Current" column, enter the amounts you now spend each year on all the expenditures listed on lines 1 to 15. Unless you carry heavy credit-card balances, the total should equal your current income. Then, estimate what your expenditures would be if you were newly retired ("Early retirement" column) and then retired but over 75 years of age ("Late retirement" column). Use today's dollars; the second worksheet takes inflation into account.

Here are simple guidelines for filling out each line of this worksheet:

Line 1. Housing will probably cost you just as much as it does now. Most retirees stay put in the same house, so they face the same property taxes and costs of homeowners' insurance, utilities and repairs. If you figure your mortgage will be paid off by then, or that you will be moving to a smaller house in a less expensive setting, take that into consideration. On the other hand, many retirees go from owning one home to taking on the responsibilities for two. If it's too early to decide on such matters, it's safe to simply assume that your post-retirement housing costs will be the same as your pre-retirement ones.

Line 2: Food costs are a major variable in retirees' budgets. That is because you can easily cut 25% from your food bill by not paying for your lunch at work five times a week. On the other hand, many retirees find that eating out becomes a major form of entertainment. And even counting early-bird specials and other discounts, restaurant meals almost always cost far more than eating at home. One way to predict your behavior after retirement is to gauge your enthusiasm for eating out now. If you are already a devoted restaurant goer, figure that you will be even more committed to the practice when you have more time. In that case, you might want to add 10% to 25% to your present bill when filling in line 2.

Line 3: Transportation costs will go down. You can subtract your commuting bill from your current account and maybe even a car if you now operate more than one.

Line 4: Taxes could represent your biggest saving of all, particularly if you don't work after you retire. First, you won't be paying the 7.65% Social Security and Medicare tax on wages any more. Besides that, you might qualify for the exemptions some states allow on taxation of Social Security benefits and pensions. In general, though, as time goes on it is wise to expect these breaks to get rarer as budget-cutting federal and state governments look for more sources of revenue. Just recall how up to 85% of retirees' Social Security benefits are currently federally taxable, depending on income.

Line 5: Medical expenses. If your employer is now paying for most everything, you'll probably have to figure on a big new expense if you retire too early for Medicare to kick in at 65. Coverage for a married couple, for instance, can run $6,000 a year. And while no one can know precisely what their medical expenses will be, it's safe to assume that the older you get the more attention you'll need. Experts advise that to cover yourself generally you should add 25% to 30% to your pre-retirement medical expenses.

Line 6: Clothing and personal-care items. You can figure on cutting this bill by 30% or 40% if you are leaving a formal office setting and entering a world of jeans and sweats.

Lines 7 and 8: Recreation and travel costs can both go up so much after retirement that they may threaten to wipe out most of your other economies. More and more, early retirement is a time of intense travel and recreation. But later retirement usually is a time of quiet and very modest travel and recreational activities.

Line 9: Education. The earlier you retire, the heavier the load might be in this area, since many early retirees have college-age children. If you will be lucky enough to be past that by then, you still might want to add an amount to cover your own course-taking, a fast-growing activity for seniors.

Line 10: Support of relatives may be nothing or it may be thousands of dollars if you have to pay for the care of your aged parents or if you decide to help your kids buy a house or pay for *their* kids' education.

Line 11: Loan and credit-card payments should be next to non-existent when you retire. Any serious debt should be paid down before you stop working.

Line 12: Insurance. Life insurance costs should be less after you retire and disability insurance should be unnecessary when you no longer have wages to protect.

Line 13: Savings and investments, contrary to what many people think, should not end with retirement. Since this is the principal way of combatting inflation and you have to expect to be exposed to it for 30 years or more, experts recommend that you plan to save 5% to 10% of your income annually during the first decade or so of retirement.

Line 14: Gifts and contributions. It makes great sense financially and emotionally to cut back on your cash donations to charities after retirement and substitute volunteering.

EXPENDITURE	CURRENT	EARLY RETIREMENT	LATE RETIREMENT
1. **Housing** (rent, mortgage, utilities, property taxes, upkeep, furnishings, homeowner's insurance premiums)			
2. **Food** (include alcohol and tobacco)			
3. **Transportation** (include car-loan payments, insurance, gas, repairs, parking and commuting costs)			
4. **Taxes** (don't include Social Security taxes after you retire unless you expect to work)			
5. **Medical and dental** (include insurance premiums, out-of-pocket expenses, prescriptions and glasses)			
6. **Clothing and personal-care items**			
7. **Recreation and hobbies**			

EXPENDITURE	CURRENT	EARLY RETIRE-MENT	LATE RETIRE-MENT
8. **Travel**			
9. **Education** (include savings for your child's education)			
10. **Support of relatives**			
11. **Loan and credit-card payments**			
12. **Life and disability insurance**			
13. **Savings and investments**			
14. **Gifts and contributions**			
15. **Other**			
TOTAL EXPENDITURES			
% OF TODAY'S INCOME NEEDED	100%		
(divide total expenditures by your current income and multiply the result by 100)			

HOW MUCH YOU MUST SAVE

Once you have estimated what percentage of your pre-retirement income you will need after you retire, you can turn to the worksheet of worksheets, the one small but indispensable chore that will point you on the road to financial independence. This one will determine how much you need to set aside each year to reach your ultimate goal.

To fill out the entire nine lines of the worksheet, you will need estimates of both Social Security benefits you expect to receive after you turn 62 and any company pensions you may be vested in. (Today's early retirees collect 80% of their full benefits if they start getting their checks at age 62; the full amount kicks in if you start receiving checks at 65. But the 80% figure drops to 75% in 2005 and to 70% in 2022 as the age for full benefits rises from the current 65 to 67.) While the Social Security Administration will make a projection for you, it may not be so easy to get a fix on your pension payout if you are not within a decade or so of retirement. In any case, your employer's benefits department may be willing to make a projection if you ask. If not, you can do some rough calculations on your own. Figure that your pension will replace about 30% of your final pre-retirement pay, based on your years of service to the company and the average of your salary over the three to five highest-paying years on the job. Your company may have a simplified formula you can use to do your calculation.

When you finish the worksheet, you will almost certainly find that your Social Security benefit and your pension together do not cover your retirement income needs. That may have been true once, but not any more, thanks to the long, active retirements most people can expect. The shortfall is the challenge presented to you by this worksheet. You have to save and invest enough to make up that gap. The faster you do so, the earlier you can retire.

A couple of points before you start. We have adapted the worksheet from a retirement education program called "How to Retire Rich," which was developed by the Seattle accounting firm of Moss Adams. The worksheet assumes that you will live to 92, 10 years more than the current 17-year life expectancy for a 65-year-old. Other assumptions: your retirement account will grow 7% a year, based on historical averages for a conservative mix of stocks and bonds; and inflation will run 5% a year, in keeping with the average for the past three decades. And finally, you should recalculate this worksheet every two years or so to account for any changes in your retirement plans, your investment performance, and any changes in Social Security or your pension.

1. **Annual income needed at retirement** (insert the average amount of current income required in early and late retirement from the worksheet above or use 80% of your current income) ________

2. **Estimated Social Security and pension** (Call Social Security at 800-772-1213 for a projection of your annual benefit. Ask your employer's benefits office to estimate your annual pension in today's dollars. Enter the total of both here.) ________

3. **Annual retirement income needed from savings and investments** (line 1 minus line 2) ________

4. **What you must save by retirement** (line 3 times factor A below) ________

5. **What you've already saved** (Total of A, B and C below) ________

    A. IRAs and Keoghs ________

    B. Vested amounts in employer savings plan ________

    C. All other investments ________

6. **Projected value of your current savings at retirement** (line 5 times factor B below) ________

7. **Total retirement capital you need to accumulate** (line 4 minus line 6) ________

8. **Annual savings needed to reach your goal** (line 7 times factor C below) ________

9. **What you must save each year until retirement** (line 8 minus the amounts you expect your employer to contribute annually to your company savings plans)

AGE AT RETIREMENT:	55	56	57	58	59	60	61	62	63	64	65
FACTOR A:	23.3	22.9	22.6	22.2	21.8	21.4	21.0	20.5	20.1	19.6	19.2

YEARS TO RETIREMENT:	1	3	6	9	12	15	20	25	30
FACTOR B:	1.03	1.09	1.18	1.29	1.40	1.53	1.76	2.02	2.33
FACTOR C:	1.000	0.324	0.155	0.099	0.071	0.054	0.038	0.028	0.022

Source: The Personal Finance Network, Moss Adams Seattle, Washington. Used by permission.

CHAPTER 4

HOW TO EVALUATE A BUYOUT

HUNDREDS OF THOUSANDS OF CORPORATE EMPLOYEES have received those tantalizing and frightening offers in recent years: give up your job and get a package of rewards in return. As both corporate and government downsizing continues, hundreds of thousands more will have to entertain buyout bids in the coming years. Depending on your situation and the size and quality of the offer that may come your way, accepting it could be the answer to all your retirement dreams, or the worst move in your financial lifetime. It all depends.

The first thing to consider is the timing of such an offer in the context of your income-producing career. If a great offer comes just a few years before you were going to retire anyway, fine. But what if you're tempted with a buyout 10 or 20 years before you're ready to call it quits? Then you have to look beyond the glittering gift to whether you can find a job that pays as well as the one you're giving up.

For more and more "RIFfed" (for reduction in force) employees, the terrifying truth is that if you're over 40 you may never be able to replace the pay you're getting now. It's true that the growing army of temporary professional and management workers often earn as much or more as staff people, but they get not a cent of benefits—

no retirement accounts, no health care coverage. After all, the value of benefits can add the equivalent of a third or more to your compensation.

Another fact of life these days: buyouts are getting skimpier. In fact, the downsizing of early-out offers themselves is used by companies as an incentive to get people to take the current buyout or face a smaller one the next time. Experts estimate that those most likely to face buyouts are employees over 55 who are in a shrinking business like retailing or defense. Such people have about a one in four chance of having to deal with such an offer.

EARLY OUT VS. VOLUNTARY SEPARATION

There are actually two types of buyout and the first (the early retirement offer) is usually a lot more generous than the second (the voluntary-separation package).

Early-retirement offers typically are aimed at employees who are 50 years of age or older. Many include a generous plumping up of pensions. For example, your employer may add from two to five years to your age or length of service or both in computing your traditional defined-benefit pension. (Your 401(k) is another matter.) So-called five-and-five offers (adding five years to your age and to your service) were common in the '80s, when companies were far more generous in these offers than they have become since. Today two-and-two deals are more the standard. And it's likely that this will seem wildly generous in a few years from now.

Another common feature of early-out offers is bridging,in which a company adds an amount to your pension (say from 60 to 62), roughly equivalent to the annual amount you will begin receiving from Social Security when you reach 62. This has the effect of having Social Security kick in, partially at least, at 60. Alas, it is also being axed by corporations looking to cut expenses. So if you're planning on retiring a decade or more from now, it might be wise not to count on a bridge even if your employer currently offers one. A general word of caution: since early-retirement packages are by far the more expensive form of buyout and are subject to complex government antidiscrimination rules, compensation experts predict that they will be seen less and less in the future.

Voluntary-separation deals, in effect, are already becoming the standard form of buyout. These can range from a pittance to a princely sum, but, as with everything corporate these days, don't let your expectations run wild. The standard lately has been one to three weeks' salary for each year of service, often cutting off at one year's pay. Here's how to size up this type of offer: Two weeks, reasonable; three weeks, excellent; and that rare offer of four weeks, solid gold.

Health insurance is an issue here for employees too young to be considered early retirees. In that case, a good deal might be a year's continued health coverage. But many voluntary-separation offers end your health coverage as soon as you leave the payroll. Under federal law, however, you are entitled to stay on in your employer's medical plan for 18 months at your own expense. After that, you'll have to look for private coverage until your are old enough to qualify for Medicare at 65. And if you're over 50, individual insurance could cost you $5,000 a year. Also be careful if you live in a state where insurers can turn you down if you are not as physically fit at they require.

MAKING THE TOUGH CHOICE

If you're closing in on retirement, even a not-so-good buyout offer may be worth taking. This is particularly true if the value of the buyout is about equal to the amount of pay you would make by staying on that extra year or two.

But what, as noted above, if you're years away from retirement? Then any offer—and not just a generous one—will require careful, even shrewd consideration. Your first question should be: does management *want* me to take this offer? While no one is forcing you to accept it, turning it down could lead you to wish you had taken it. The company could follow up with a period of harassment, demotion, pay cuts, and even job elimination. To head off this hell, look for signs that may tell you whether you're wanted or not.

The best indicator is your boss. Does he appear happy with your performance? Not over the long term, but your recent performance? If his attitude toward you appears to have grown negative in any way, you may have to connect that with the buyout and conclude that you are expected to leave. Also find out, if possible, whether the buyout is aimed at a specific department or job title. And if that includes you, perhaps you should think about saying yes to the offer. You will likely have only two or three months to think the offer over, so make the best of that time.

What, then, if you are pretty sure you are not one of those targeted for the door, but the offer may be too generous to pass up? That's when you need to look beyond this job and determine whether you really can afford to let go of it. After all, your employer wants you to stay. So the next question is: How far will the buyout plus my other assets take me? If the answer is not nearly far enough to cover the rest of your life, you then have to take a hard look at your employment prospects. If the job outlook is healthy or you have realistic plans to set up your own business, you may want to grab the offer even if it is not the most generous you've ever heard of.

One more thing to think about is the bigger pension you would get if you stayed on at your present job. Study the table below, which demonstrates the dramatic differences between taking a buyout at 55 and staying on with the pension clock ticking until 65. Our example is a 55-year-old earning $50,000 a year with 20 years' service for a company. The buyout offer adds five years to both his age and years of service. That yields a pension the worker would not normally receive until he turned 60. He also gets an extra $6,800 for seven years as a bridge to Social Security, which kicks in at age 62 and pays a third more than the bridge stipend.

You can see in the table that by turning down the buyout and working until 60 or 62, the employee would raise his retirement income by as much as $8,891 a year. That's $6,891 in additional pension, $1,600 from his heftier 401(k) and $400 from his bigger Social Security check.

AGE	INCOME WITH RETIREMENT AT 55 WITHOUT THE PACKAGE	INCOME WITH RETIREMENT AT 55 WITH THE PACKAGE	INCOME WITH RETIREMENT AT AGE 60	INCOME WITH RETIREMENT AT AGE 62
55	$9,703	$21,177	$51,500	$51,500
60	9,703	21,177	17,354	59,700
62	19,273	24,577	27,754	33,468
65	19,273	24,577	27,754	33,468

Note: The table assumes that the employee's pension is based on his five highest years of earnings, that he gets 3% annual pay raises, and that he contributes 3% of his salary to his 401(k), which he annuitizes at retirement. Social Security kicks in at 62. **Source: Kwasha Lipton**

What, then, is an employee determined to retire young and rich to do if a reasonable buyout offer comes along? The smartest strategy is to be prepared by having your next step in your career all plotted out. Do you have live leads to your next job if it comes to that? Or do you have realistic prospects for starting your own business? If not, you may be in no position to take the money and run. And that would be a shame if the offer is a tempting one.

CHAPTER 5

HOW TO INVEST FOR YOUR FUTURE

HERE IS WHERE YOU'LL REALLY BE PUT TO THE TEST. Up to this point, basically you've been asked to do two things: first, make sure you are saving enough from your income; and second, set your annual savings goal. If you haven't accomplished both, you're not ready to concentrate on investing. The groundwork just hasn't been done. On the first point, you can't invest properly if you don't have the money put aside to invest with. On the second, you have to know where you're going and if you've come far enough along each year.

So let's say you're ready for the next step. Perhaps you are already an investor. Maybe you have even owned some stocks and mutual funds. But if you're like most people, you haven't established any sense of order in your investing. Without a doubt, the temptation to invest randomly is greater than ever. There are more influences than ever trying to get you to buy stocks, bonds, mutual funds, and dozens of other kinds of investments. Tips and rumors of hot stocks are rampant, as TV and newspapers wade deeper and deeper into investment reporting. Many people, enticed by articles and ads touting the latest hot mutual fund, wind up after a few years with perhaps a dozen funds with no coordination among them.

If you fall into this class of fund consumer, chances are you have a huge problem of redundancy among your funds. Sure, some of them are so-called large-cap funds that buy only huge corporations, while some may be small-cap funds that stay with up-and-comers. But there is more to diversification among funds than that. For instance, do you know which of your stock funds are growth funds and which are value funds? Which are equity-income? Got any mid-caps? And how about the balance of industries among your stock funds? Many fund managers are enamored of technology stocks, for instance. If all or most of your stock funds have big commitments to technology, the next time that sector takes a dive, most of your wonderfully diversified funds will plunge too.

Then there's the question of growth vs. income. The 1980s saw a long bull market in bonds. It was so long that many younger investors weren't aware that there was ever much downside in bond investing. Then came the bust of the early '90s and one of investing's cyclical lessons was learned again. What was so sad for many investors, in fact, was that they were probably too young to be in bond funds in the first place. Growth should be the primary, maybe even the sole, emphasis of any investor who is more than a few years away from retirement. And for those who expect to retire early, young and rich, growth is just about the only way to go. But you have to do it in a reasoned, orderly way. And that's the first lesson in this lesson-heavy chapter on investing.

IT'S ASSET ALLOCATION, STUPID

And it's really simple. Just make sure you select a portfolio with the right mix of stocks and bonds, and make careful adjustments every 10 years or so. That's it. And here is why this rule is so overarchingly important. Most of your profit from investing comes directly from getting the right combination of assets. A seminal 1991 study by money managers Gary P. Brinson and Brian D. Singer and consultant Gilbert Beebower found that about 92% of investor returns comes from asset allocation. The other 8%, astonishingly, comes from picking the right stock, bond or fund and from the correct timing of your buying and selling.

BASIC RULES FOR ALL AGES

As you'll see below, you should shift your asset allocations as you get older. But some aspects of your investing ought to stay solid and unchanging, like beacons. There are five:

1) Make stocks your number one investment. As you move through this chapter and see how we recommend you allocate your money to different investments, one thing may startle you: that stocks dominate the mix. Let's make clear right now how important this insight is. Since 1926, stocks on average have whipped the competition by a huge margin: stocks have on average returned 10.3% a year before taxes, compared with 5% for long-term Treasury bonds, and only 3.1% for cash investments like short-term Treasury bills. That last performance is just in line with inflation, which means that cash didn't really return anything over nearly 70 years. Yet poll after poll shows that the average U.S. household invests only about a quarter of its assets in stocks, half the amount it puts into fixed-income assets like bonds. That means that just on the basis of general choice, the average American family is gaining only half as much as it should with its investments. And if asset allocation is not being done correctly, and you have to assume that in most homes it isn't, Americans by and large are getting only a fraction of the bang out of their investment dollar that they should. That's a formula for retiring old and insecure. And it's sad, because it is totally unnecessary.

2) Invest through mutual funds. To follow our asset allocation guidelines with stocks and bonds requires the time, talent and knowledge of markets that few individual investors possess. The fact of the matter is that few investors are interested enough in the stock market alone to make the needed investment of time. So don't kid yourself, or be persuaded by some posturing stock jockey, that you can do it all yourself. Besides, some categories of investment—particularly international stocks and bonds, and to a lesser extent small stocks and bonds in general—are best approached via mutual funds. For instance, it is difficult to follow most foreign stocks easily; and the high volatility of small stocks calls for constant monitoring. Instead, go for the diversification and professional management of mutual funds. (For more on buying individual funds, see the following chapter.)

3) Stay the course. As we've already said, the overexposure in the media and generalized hype associated with mutual fund investing is one of the underappreciated reasons why many investors fail to make steady, sizable progress in their returns. The fund of the moment looks tantalizing and the fund you already own sometimes looks bedraggled by comparison.

So why not switch out of your fund and into the winner? Because today's hero will be tomorrow's nobody. Count on it. Several recent studies indicate that people who buy load funds (those with a sales commission that can range to 5% or more) made as much as 20% more over the past 10 years than those who bought no-load funds. This would seem impossible unless managers of load funds are inherently more talented stock pickers than managers of no-load funds.

The real reason for the gap in performance: the load fund customers stayed with their funds largely because they had paid a stiff entry fee and didn't want to just throw it away. The no-load customers, on the other hand, felt freer to dump their funds as market conditions changed and other funds looked more enticing. So if you've chosen your funds well, there is rarely a reason to sell. And since most investors sell when an investment is down, selling usually means losing. Take to heart this sobering observation from Benjamin Graham, one of the guiding geniuses of stock investing: "The investor's chief problem—and even his worst enemy—is himself."

4) Put everything you can into your 401(k). Or your Individual Retirement Account (IRA), Keogh, 403(b) or other tax-deferred retirement plan. Because the money you put into one is usually not taxed, and particularly because that money is then allowed to compound untaxed until you take it out after retirement, these plans are by far the best place to have your investments.

This example is dramatic evidence: Say you saved $5,000 a year for 30 years, got an 8% rate of return each year and paid taxes at 28%. After the 30 years, your fund would be worth $288,585. But if instead you put that same $5,000 into a 401(k) plan at work each year and received the same 8% return, you would wind up with $611,729—more than double the amount earned outside the tax-deferred account. And since most employers who offer 401(k) plans also match your contribution with one of their own—say, 50 cents on the dollar—the typical account would grow even faster than the example shows.

5) Allocate *all* of your investments. A common error people make is forgetting one or more portions of his or her entire portfolio of investments when figuring out asset allocation. Let's say, for instance, that you are concentrating your saving or investing on a company 401(k). But you may also have a separate account holding company stock that you have been accumulating. Or you have a fund, an annuity or maybe even a stash of U.S. savings bonds. Include every last one of these investments when you compute your asset allocation or else your portfolio will be out of balance.

Now for the nitty-gritty. Following are four model portfolios of investments that will yield a well balanced asset-allocation mix—for your 20s to 30s, 30s to 40s, 40s to 50s and 50s to 60s.

PORTFOLIO 1: 20S TO EARLY 30S
ASSET MIX:
10% large-company stocks
25% midcap stocks
15% small-company stocks
30% international stocks
15% intermediate-term corporate bonds
5% convertible or high-yield bonds

As you can see from the above table, we are recommending that the youngest investors should put no less than 80% of their money into stock funds. Since in this phase you are furthest away from needing retirement money to live on, it makes perfect sense to put a maximum amount into the kind of investment that pays best over time.

Remember that when you are diversified and your investments are being carefully shepherded by professional mutual fund managers, you may face some frightening short-term losses along the way, but in the long run you will do best with stocks. So let's take this advice a step further: if you can make it through the occasional stock market storms without losing sleep, by all means increase your stock allocation to 100% while you are young. You have nothing to lose but a few more years of your working life. You have nothing to gain but an earlier retirement.

If you are a true novice at investing, and you have only $1,000 or so to start you off, your best bet is to buy just one fund that holds large-company stocks and has a good long-term performance record under the same manager. (Again, more on buying a fund in Chapter 6.) If stocks make you nervous, be aware that this type of fund collects blue chips that don't have the stomach-churning volatility of smaller, less tested stocks. But let's say you want to get your feet wet with a stock fund that's even tamer than that. In such a case, seek out a balanced or asset-allocation fund. Both these categories of fund split their holdings between stocks and bonds; the bonds are like ballast shielding the overall portfolio from the risk even a blue-chip stock fund faces. But as you gain experience as a stock investor, and as you see what goes down come up again and make real headway, chances are you will become less risk-averse. When that happens, move back into the pure-stock funds where the ride, though bumpier, is far more rewarding.

When your stash grows to the $10,000 level, it's time to branch out into midcaps (stocks of companies with annual revenues from $1 billion to $5 billion) and small caps (those with revenues of $1 billion or less). With 25% in midcaps, 15% in small caps, 30% in international funds and only 10% in the more stable large-cap funds, you can see what is happening. You are not simply diversifying; you are extending your risk. The reason is that the highest returns in the coming years are widely expected to come in smaller stocks and those of other nations.

Historically, in fact, small stocks have outpaced larger ones, with average annual returns of 12.4% vs. 10.3% for blue chips.

International stocks have soared and ebbed in recent years, making them considerably more volatile than domestic shares. When you begin buying international funds, then, consider again your stomach for churning markets, because you have to expect a high level of volatility on this front for the foreseeable future. Currency swings alone can be a huge factor that you don't have to face if you keep to domestic stocks funds. But as the global economy asserts itself, experts assert that there will be nowhere to hide from the presence of world stocks—not, at least, if you are out to achieve big returns over the coming years. One recommendation: as you start out, stay away from so-called emerging-market funds—those that specialize in such developing economies as Latin America and the smaller countries of the Far East. But since the stocks of those countries are widely expected to offer the most sensational growth opportunities of the next few decades, remember that as you get more used to market dips and as your nestegg grows, you may well want to add one or more such funds to your mix later on.

One more complication on the stock front for now: get to know which of your funds are value and which are growth funds. As you get older, you will probably want to have both types in your portfolio because each brings a particular strength. Value funds buy out-of-favor stocks with prices that do not fully reflect their real value. Growth-stock funds go for stocks with fast-growing earnings, even if they feature premium prices. Over time, the value style of investing tends to outperform the growth style by a couple of pecentage points. But no one knows when the stock market will be responding to value and when it will be geared to growth.

One sensible recommendation: try to keep about 60% of your stock allocation in value funds and the rest in growth funds. When newspapers and magazines report on mutual fund performance, they often indicate which style each stock fund follows.

And now a word about your fixed-income allocation. As the table indicates, put 15% of your money in investment-grade bonds, those with intermediate maturities of five to 10 years. This segment of the mix is the solidest and least volatile of all. In fact, studies have shown that intermediates yield returns virtually as good as those of 30-year bonds with only half the volatility.

Think of this portion as the ballast of your portfolio. Then things get a bit racy with the rest of the fixed-income allocation, putting 5% of your money into either a convertible bond fund or a high-yield bond fund. The first offers a good chance at capital gains when bonds the fund owns are "converted" into common stock. The second increases your risk via portfolios of "junk" bonds; diversification and careful picking can increase your yields to more than 9% without the danger of buying individual junk bonds.

A special note on buying bond funds: because bonds can't reach for the kind of performance over time that stocks enjoy, buy only those bond funds with annual fees below 1%; many fine ones nick you very gently, at less than 0.5%. And stick with no-load funds in this category. You can find all the relevant information on fees and charges in each fund's prospectus, or in fund listings in major newspapers and magazines.

Bottom line: Over several years, you can figure on how well your portfolio will perform during this initial phase of your investment life. Based on past returns, our configuration of 80% stocks and 20% bonds is likely to increase by an annual average of 9%. Possible expected return can run as high as 25% and as low as 7% in any one year.

PORTFOLIO 2: EARLY 30S TO 40S
ASSET MIX:
10% large-company stocks
25% midcap stocks
10% small-cap stocks
25% international stocks
20% intermediate corporate bonds
10% international bonds

Going by the book, now is the time to reduce your risk somewhat, especially if you have by now taken on the responsibility of a family and a mortgage. Our table above suggests that you drop from 80% in stocks to 70%, heavying up on more stable bonds. In addition, by trimming your small-stock exposure from 15% to 10% and international stocks from 30% to 25%, you further tame down your mix.

This is as far as most people in this age group should go in recognizing the need for financial stability. After all, you still have two decades or so before normal retirement. In fact, those with more daring and less family responsibility might even want to stay closer to the 80%-stock guideline laid down for the youngest group.

If you follow the allocation to the letter, you will be switching the money you have just trimmed from stocks into your intermediate-term bond fund, which would grow from 15% to 20% of the portfolio.

On the fixed-income side, you'll notice that an international bond fund has been added as 10% of the portfolio as a diversification note, standing in for the more daring high-yield or convertible fund. The international exposure in bonds is strongly diversifying because fixed-income markets in the U.S. and abroad tend to move in different directions. The risk here is of the foreign exchange variety. Even disinterested Americans have gotten used to headlines in the TV evening news and in the morning papers about the dollar sinking against the Japanese yen or the German mark. But again, if your money rides the wavy foreign-exchange markets for a good decade or so, you should more than make up for the occasional dip and dive.

Bottom line: You should look for average annual returns of about 8.75%, with a risk of losing up to 5.75% and a chance of gaining as much as 23.25% in any single year.

PORTFOLIO 3: EARLY 40S TO 50S
ASSET MIX:
20% large-company stocks
20% midcap stocks
10% small-company stocks
20% international stocks
25% intermediate Treasuries/munis
5% international bonds

While your overall split remains at 70% stocks, 30% bonds, some small rejiggering leaves you somewhat safer. This is as it should be: you are getting older and closer to retirement; and you are likely experiencing the tightest family-budget period, thanks to college bills. Lowering your risk soothes your nerves and guards your winnings so far. But you still have plenty of growth in your mix because your added safety is accomplished primarily by doubling the proportion of large-cap blue chips to 20% from 10% and dropping both midcaps and international stocks from 25% to 20%.

Another way to increase the stability of your portfolio is by tilting the stock portion away from growth funds and toward both value funds and equity-income funds. By going for low-priced stocks, value funds normally don't fall as far as growth funds when the stock market takes a tumble. The same is true of equity-income funds, which fall less than growth funds largely because they tend to buy more stable dividend-paying stocks. There's a price to be paid for all this peaceableness, of course: when the bull market is roaring ahead, value and equity-income entrants don't rise as fast or as high as pure growth stocks.

On the bond front, you can lock in the ultimate in safety by moving completely out of corporates and cutting the internationals in half and putting the proceeds—fully a quarter of your entire portfolio—into Treasury notes. These are U.S. Treasury issues ranging in maturity from one to 10 years. Depending on the direction of the bond market at any given time, Treasury notes yield nearly as much as 30-year Treasury bonds without the long-term commitment and consequent higher volatility. And usually it is a better idea to forego the management fees associated with Treasury bond funds and go directly for the notes themselves. (You can buy them through a brokerage house or save even that fee and go directly to the seller, the Federal Reserve. For information, call 202-452-3000 or your local Federal Reserve branch.)

An alternative to Treasury notes would be a municipal bond fund for investors in the 28% federal tax bracket or above. Again, look for muni funds with annual fees that are well under 1% and that hold bonds rated A or better.

Bottom line: Heavying up on large-cap stocks will hold your probable risk of loss to 5% and permit a possible gain of as much as 21% in any year. Average returns: 8%.

PORTFOLIO 4: EARLY 50S TO 60S
ASSET MIX:
20% large-cap stocks
15% midcap stocks
5% small-company stocks
20% international stocks
40% muni bonds or T-notes

If you were lucky enough to consult, say, your grandparents at this point in your life, you might receive priceless pieces of wisdom about the art of aging gracefully. But when they got to finances, you would probably receive truly bum advice—heartfelt but nonetheless bad. They would no doubt tell you that now is the time to convert all of your assets into bank certificates of deposit or at most supersafe bonds like those issued by the U.S. Treasury. You could forgive them for being wrong, because when they retired they could reasonably look forward to a fairly limited number of golden years. But since you are looking at 30 or more of those years, getting rid of your growth investments would almost certainly ensure that you run out of money long before you die, unless you are a multimillionaire. And for anyone contemplating really early retirement—before 55 or so—such a move would be a long-term disaster, considering that any fixed-income investment or pension would be worth just half as much in 15 years if inflation runs only a modest 4% annually.

So you'll still need growth and lots of it. That's why our asset allocation model, while dropping from 70% in stocks, will still maintain a 60-40 balance between stocks and fixed-income instruments. Large-cap stocks hold at 20%, as do internationals; but midcaps drop from 20% to 15% and small-cap exposure is cut in half from 10% to 5%.

As a further bow to safety, the entire 40% income allocation is swept into U.S. Treasury notes or municipal bonds.

Bottom line: Our model portfolio shoots for average annual returns of 7.5%, with risk of loss averaging 4.5% and possible gain ranging as high as 19.5% in any year.

Now that you know how much of which kinds of funds you should own at each stage in your life, the next step is selecting the right specific funds. We turn to that question in the next chapter.

CHAPTER 6

HOW TO CHOOSE MUTUAL FUNDS

IT'S OFTEN SAID that investments aren't bought, they're sold. If you've ever been on the receiving end of a "cold call" from a hungry young stockbroker, you know the story. Salesmen or ads or hyped newspaper articles can steamroll you into buying more out of excited ignorance than dispassionate knowledge. And that insight applies as much to mutual funds as to any stock, bond or other investment.

Today there are over 7,000 mutual funds you can buy—more than the total number of stocks traded on the New York Stock Exchange and the American Stock Exchange combined. Brokers use this profusion and resulting confusion as a lever. Their argument: there are just too many funds for the individual to decide what to buy. Then—surprise!—you wind up being sold funds marketed by the very brokerage house that employs the broker who is selling you the funds. Some choice. Or you read the breathless stories that appear in newspapers and magazines four times a year describing the latest "hot" funds; then you run out and buy them. But next year they're not hot anymore and you go through the same cycle, jettisoning last year's heroes and grabbing onto this year's.

That's no way to be an investor. In the long run you wind up either losing money or at least not making as much as you should. And, of course, missing out on the opportunity to retire young and rich. The aim of this chapter is to teach you enough about mutual funds so that you can either buy them yourself or at least be able to monitor buying and selling by your financial adviser. (See Chapter 8 for advice on choosing an adviser.)

THE IDEAL: TO BUY AND TO HOLD

Unless you are a close student of mutual fund activity who spends hours every week checking out market shifts, comings and goings of fund managers and other vital fund news, join the majority of mutual fund investors: those who sincerely want their money to grow but lack the interest and time to manage that growth. Isn't that what you're paying the fund managers to do anyway? If that fairly describes you, common sense tells you that you had better buy your funds with care, because you will be leaving them in the hands of their managers for long stretches of time during which you will be proccupied with many other facets of your life.

Buy and hold, in fact, has long been honored by some of the most astute students of the stock market. And if it's a viable approach to stock investing, it should be even more so when it comes to stock funds. A stock, for instance, can fall prey to any number of problems that demand that you sell it. But a well managed fund that is part of a well run fund family, even if it never leads the list of performers in any one year, ought to bring excellent returns over time.

Unfortunately, the situation is considerably stickier when it comes to bond funds. One of the safest investment moves you can make is to buy a high-quality bond, hold it to maturity, receive your interest along the way and get your principal back at the end. No interest rate risk because the rate is set and predictable when you buy. No market risk because you are willing to wait out the term of the bond and not try to sell in the hurly burly of the bond market, which is subject to unpredictable interest rate fluctuations. But when you get into a bond fund, whose managers buy and sell bonds all the time, you are subject to market risk *and* interest rate risk. So it's at least as essential that you place your money with bond funds whose managers have demonstrated their ability to come out ahead over time.

The rest of this chapter relates the most important points to look for and the major pitfalls to avoid when buying a fund. It ends with a short and to-the-point discussion of when you should give up and sell a fund.

LOADS, NO LOADS AND FEES

How much should you pay a mutual fund for its services? Too few investors take this issue seriously. Why worry about a few percentage points, they reason, when you're making an easy 15%, 20% or more each year in the market? Not many stock market specialists believe that we'll see anything like that again.That is why you should take a closer look at total return—your profit when everything is taken into account. That's not just gains in the market and dividends from stock funds; not just gains in the market and interest in bond funds. But all income added up and costs subtracted.

This leads us to the noisiest running feud in the entire world of mutual funds: should you buy load funds or no-load funds? No-loads, for those just starting out, are mutual funds that you buy directly from the fund company without any load or sales charge. Load funds, by contrast, are those that are sold by stockbrokers or financial planners, who collect a sales charge typically around 4.5%, but running as high as 8.5%.

If you study history, you could go crazy trying to determine which has done better, loads or no-loads. If you're wise, you will come away with the conviction that the load factor has nothing at all to do with fund performance. A study by Morninstar Inc. came up with the eight most dependable funds in America—the eight stock funds that beat the three- and five-year increases of the benchmark

Standard & Poor's 500 Index and of the average equity fund. Four were loads, four were no-loads.

So what should you do now? It depends to a surprising extent on how disciplined an investor you are. That's because of two key factors, one favoring loads and the other favoring no-loads.

Buy load funds if you think you are apt to be so frightened by a market drop or so smitten by the next hot fund of the month that you'll keep shifting in and out of different funds. This, as we've said, is the surest way to lose money. And what is so instructive is that recent studies indicate that people invested in load funds, because they have committed to hefty sales charges, tend to stay put longer than no-load investors, who are much more apt to flit about. And that explains why so many people do so much better in load funds over time.

Buy no-load funds if you can maintain discipline while others panic. The reason is simple: if no-loads are just as good as loads, why pay the sales charge? Particularly these days, when profits won't be coming as fast and thick as they were in the '80s, putting the equivalent of a sales charge to work as part of your investment can make a real difference.

Management fees can be an even greater expense than loads if you hold a fund for a number of years. So the argument above about getting as much of your money into the investment itself and not losing it through expenses goes doubly here. In general, try to keep the annual management fee on your stock funds, particularly large-caps and midcaps, below 1%. Among stock funds, you can make an exception for small-stock funds and international funds, which are generally more expensive to run. But have a strong reason for going above 1.3% on a small-cap and 1.5% on diversified international stock funds. As for bond funds, the rule is even stricter: with few exceptions, avoid any with annual fees that exceed .9%. As you look around, in fact, you will find highly regarded stock and bond funds with fees under 1/2 or even 1/4 of 1%. Also try to stay clear of funds that feature **12b-1 fees**, which are annual charges that pay for a fund's marketing costs and that can skim off an additional .15% to 1% of your money. Load funds are where you are apt to find 12b-1 fees:

nearly nine out of 10 broker-sold funds carry them. But nearly three out of 10 no-loads also charge 12b-1s.

REGULATING RISK

By following asset-allocation models like the ones we showed you in Chapter 5, you are going far in establishing the amount of risk that is right for you. For instance, you'll never stray too far into the more volatile types of stock funds, the internationals and the small caps. And you'll have the ballast of bonds increasing as you get older. We have also steered you to safer and safer bond or fixed-income choices along the way.

But you can do a considerable amount of fine-tuning of your risk as you go about choosing individual stock funds to buy. You can do this by selecting, say, one large-cap fund over another because it has a bit more risk and therefore promises more of a reward in your total return. Or conversely, you can go for the less risky fund if you feel more comfortable reining in risk as you go along.

You also have a range of stock fund types aside from large caps, midcaps and small caps. Here's a rundown:

Growth funds are the riskiest of all, but over the long term they get the best results. They invest in the stocks of companies the fund managers expect to grow fast and that normally plow earnings back into growth instead of into shareholder dividends. You need to have the stomach to ride out the occasional plunges these funds take without panicking and selling out. The most speculative of this category are often referred to as aggressive-growth funds, often specializing in small-cap stocks.

Total-return funds try to achieve steady returns from a combination of capital gains and interest or dividends. As a result such funds behave more smoothly than growth funds, dropping less in down markets but rising less in up markets. Total-return funds comprise three sub-categories of fund. Starting with the riskiest, they are growth and income, equity income and supercautious balanced funds, which invest in a combination of safe dividend-paying stocks and bonds.

Value funds, as noted in the previous chapter, look for undervalued stocks. In style, their managers stand in contrast to growth-fund managers. Value funds can be found among those that buy small-cap, midcap, large-cap, domestic and international stocks. Most investors don't get deeply enough into the study of stocks to decide whether they favor the growth style or the value style, which is fine. All you need to know is that both are perfectly valid, that the market tends to favor one style over the other at different times, and that therefore as your wad grows it would be wise to have some of both in your portfolio.

HOW MANY FUNDS?

One of the least talked-about addictions of post-industrial American life is not being able to stop buying mutual funds. Everybody seems to be looking for the Magellan of the '90s, the successor to the famous growth fund that had a spectacular run during the '80s under the management of the talented Peter Lynch. Everybody also seemed to be clamoring to get into the hottest new emerging-markets fund, the kind that invests in developing countries. Until emerging stock markets started to take dramatic dives--first when the Mexican peso fiasco trashed previously high-flying Latin American funds; then when Asian economies hit the wall.And everybody seems to be sniffing out the latest little small-cap fund or the one that successfully marries value and growth investing and on and on. You get the idea.

The outcome of all this excitement is that too many small investors who don't read much beyond the headlines in the business pages of their newspapers wind up holding dozens of mutual funds. What's wrong with that? First of all, it becomes progressively difficult to keep track of your funds. And especially if you've been buying hot ones, chances are they will cool off deeply in a year or two and lag the markets for the rest of your life if you hang onto them. Second, anyone who has more than a handful of funds will almost surely find out that they have huge overlaps that may be dangerous. For instance, many otherwise diversified funds hold huge wads of technology stocks in their portfolios. Some major funds have up to 25% of their holdings in technology stocks, two and a half times the weighting of such issues in the Standard & Poor's 500 stock index.

This not only reduces diversification, a bedrock virtue of investing in mutual funds in the first place; it also means that when one fund manager decides it's time to dump technology issues, his move could cause a stampede that could badly hurt all those funds with big commitments to these stocks. And if you're left holding only one such fund, the damage is a lot less than if you have, say, half a dozen growth funds and all of them are overweighted in tech stocks.

Experts advise that few investors should hold more than a dozen funds. Beginners with only a few thousand dollars to invest hardly need more than one or two. And if you follow our asset allocation suggestions in Chapter 5, you need not invest in more than half a dozen funds.

It's also wise to limit your purchases to only a couple of fund families. These are companies, such as Fidelity, T Rowe Price, Vanguard and American Century—that offer a wide selection of stock, bond and money funds. Administration and paperwork is kept to a minimum this way, and expenses can also be kept down if you do any switching among funds within the same families. Some fund families—notably Fidelity and Charles Schwab—have branched out into networks that offer hundreds of funds from dozens of different families under the same roof.

FOUR ADDED POINTS TO CONSIDER

As a long-term fund investor, you'll be happier, less nervous and all-round better off if you shrewdly choose every fund you buy. You already know you will be in the market for one or more large-cap, midcap, small-cap, and international stock funds, plus three or four kinds of bond funds. You've been clued in on loads vs. no-loads and the elements of risk. Here are four additional judgments that will help you zero in on the choicest picks:

1. **Don't overlook index funds.** These are the funds that buy all the stocks in a given index, such as the Standard & Poor's 500, and thereby mimic the performance of those stocks as a whole. Today you can buy a range of index funds for large stocks like the S&P 500, for small stocks (the Wilshire or Russell indexes), for international securities and so on. Champions of index funds like their steady if often unspectacular performance, their usually low fees, and their tendency to cost you less in taxes because of their low turnover. As your investment stake grows and you get older, you may want to turn to one or more index funds for your stock or bond asset allocations. If you do, you might consider putting your taxable money in index funds and keeping your tax-deferred 401(k)s and IRAs in actively managed funds.

2. **Do pass on sector funds.** Some of the larger fund families offer sector funds, which invest exclusively in the stocks of a single industry (like health care or technology) or commodity (like gold). These are among the most volatile funds of all, often landing at the top of the performance charts one year and at the bottom the next. They won't give you the steady advances that well diversified funds will.

3. **Ditto smart-aleck funds.** These are the ones that practice market timing, moving massively into or out of stocks according to their readings of technical indicators. No one has been able to successfully time the market over time, and market timers are a colorful example of winner-loser streaks, with emphasis on the loser. That's why you'll see feature stories in the press about the brave financial analyst who single-handedly called the latest market swing. Chances are you'll either hear no more of that momentary star, or read a year or two later that he or

she has just made a disastrously wrong market call this time.

Another variety of smart-aleck fund is the one that bets a significant proportion of its entire portfolio on a single stock. This approach to stock picking is for people with a richer taste for risk than the average investor should entertain. So if you see a fund putting 8% or more of its money on one stock, back away.

4. Stay with the track stars. As we said before, the fund stars of the moment tend to be momentary flashes. The real winners are those with the solidest long-term records. Don't consider a fund that lags over at least the past three years.

HOW TO GET ALL THAT INFO

We've laid out a healthy diet of data for you to collect--about loads and management fees, the families the funds belong to, types of funds, turnover, long-term performance records and more. Let's stop her and say this: It's not a hard job, and you don't have to be an investing nerd to absorb it. Here's how to go about it:

First off, if you are buying load funds through a broker or financial planner, or no-load funds recommended by a financial planner, *get that pro to do the spadework for you.* This is a particularly fair demand when you are dealing with a broker or planner who is about to get a fat commission for selling you the fund. This is part of his or her job, and don't do business with anyone who balks at full disclosure. (For more on choosing and dealing with a professional adviser, see Chapter 8.)

If you are doing the research yourself, you will find most of what you need in the prospectus that the fund family sends to you with your application forms. You would do well also to consult the latest quarterly performance reports that appear in major newspapers and personal finance magazines. Your local public library probably carries the magazines and may even subscribe to mutual-fund-advisory newsletters. Who knows? You might even find it all fascinating.

WHEN TO SELL

This section was nearly omitted for one very good reason: if you choose carefully, you will likely be able to hang onto your funds for the long run. That being said, the two generally valid reasons for selling a mutual fund are:

1. **Performance has been inexcusably poor.** There are many times in the life of a fund when it suffers a sinking spell. When this happens, you can't just overlook it because if it doesn't snap back your long-term retirement plans may be in trouble. The other reason for investigating is that there may be a very good and excusable reason for the drop, such as when an entire group like small-cap stocks or an approach like value investing falls into market disfavor. So if a fund you own has a one-year loss or just stagnates for a couple of years, check it out. You may find that the second reason for dumping a fund is the operative one here.

2. **There has been a change in management.** Like a restaurant with a new chef, a mutual fund with a new manager can become a wholly different entity, serving up lackluster results. It is wise to check with the fund every six months or at least once a year to see if the manager who has made the record you bought the fund for has departed. If so, call the fund family and ask straight out if the new manager plans to continue the same investing strategy. If not, and you are not happy with what you hear, it may be a signal to sell. And even if you get a pledge that the approach will not change, keep checking on performance to make sure the new person can actually carry out the fund's philosophy as well as the star he or she has replaced.

CHAPTER 7

GETTING THE MOST OUT OF SAVINGS PLANS

IT'S TIME TO TALK SERIOUSLY about the retirement savings plan that your employer offers you: your 401(k) if you're employed by a for-profit company, your 403(b) if you work for a tax-exempt organization; or even your Keogh or SEP plan if you are self-employed. Here is the central issue about these plans, and you should take a moment to let it sink in:

These are without question your number one, most powerful and important retirement savings vehicles. Yet they are badly abused and mismanaged by most people who have them. This chapter is about running your plan so it produces results equal to its capacity.

We'll explain. If you want to retire young and rich, or even at 65 with enough to live comfortably for the rest of your life, you will need a nestegg that draws from three sources. First is Social Security, but as we've seen, that will probably be the smallest part. Then there are the savings and investments you make on your own, outside your corporate savings plan. This portion will probably fall somewhere in between in size, and to be realistic for most people it will be tiny or even non-existent; most Americans just don't save that well. The third portion of your stash, the 401(k) or other tax-deferred plan, will in all likelihood be the biggest piece of your pie. (Your employer may also give you a traditional pension, but many don't and even so, that doesn't involve any saving by you.)

It's important to understand the tremendous investment energy that one of these plans unleashes. Since you are most likely to have a 401(k), we'll use that as our example, although our argument covers all of them in general. When you tell your payroll department how much to siphon from your paychecks each year into your 401(k)—the maximum allowable in 1995 is $9,240—100% of that money goes to work for you because it is untaxed.

Then many employers match your contribution at rates of 50 cents or more on the dollar. In addition, any profits—dividends, interest and capital gains–-are also untaxed until you start withdrawing money after age 59 1/2. Finally, all these dollars compound at such increasingly furious rates that in the long run more of the money in your account comes from compound interest than from the money you have been putting in. It's a bravura peformance that you could never get out of investments made outside such a protected plan.

So it's only good sense that you closely watch that 401(k) and make the decisions that will help it grow to the max. But if you're like most of the 401(k) holders polled in study after study, you are making a powerful thoroughbred trot around the track when he could be winning races. What people tend to do is to put their money into the safest options, the ones that deliver safe but modest income year after year. What they should be doing is letting most of their dough ride on growth options, which admittedly can suffer bruising short-term losses, but always come back to win big over the long term.

According to Ibbitson Associates, a highly respected financial research and consulting firm in Chicago, here are the compound average annual rates of return over 60 years ending in 1993:

Large stocks (S&P 500):	11.4%
Small stocks	15.1%
Long-term corporate bonds	5.5%
Long-term government bonds	5.1%
30-day Treasury bills	3.9%

Keeping these rates of return in mind, let's see what the difference would be over time between the conservative and the growth stash. Say you managed to put $500 a month into your tax-deferred account for 30 years. Here is what you would wind up with in your 401(k) or 403(b) or Keogh at the end:

At a 4% rate, roughly the return from keeping all your money in supersafe Treasury bills: **$458,000.**

At a 12% rate, roughly the return from keeping all your money in large-cap stocks: **$3,248,000.**

There, in a nutshell, is the path to take when your goal is to retire young and rich.

What's really so wasteful about the way people mismanage their 401(k)s is that their options have opened up dramatically in recent years, prodded by federal regulations creating incentives for companies to increase their choices. The result is that most companies with 401(k)s offer no less than four funds to choose from, and many offer 10 or more. The most common choices offered are, beginning with the least risky: government bond funds; guaranteed investment contracts (GICs), which are fixed-income instruments generally paying somewhat more than government bonds; balanced funds; equity-income funds; growth funds; and the employer's own stock. Many companies are also adding international funds, small-company funds and asset-allocation funds.

Again, however, almost as if there were a curse on self-management of investing, studies have shown that when the options grow too numerous, many employees get so confused they throw up their hands and drop out of the plans entirely. This is sad and unnecessary, because the care and feeding of a 401(k) is really quite simple if you follow a few guidelines.

Contribute as much as you can. Here is the way to invest: first max out on your 401(k). If you have tried but failed to do so, it's time to go over your budget and cut back, because this is the absolute foundation of your retirement dream. You must be putting the most you can in the plan or all bets are off; you're just not being serious. Second, when you are able to put the full amount into your 401(k), then begin building a portfolio of investments outside the plan.

Try never to take anything out of your plan. Many companies allow employees to borrow from their 401(k)s under favorable conditions. Resist this blandishment. The whole idea of a special tax-deferred account is compromised if the money in it is not compounding maximally at all times. Many people are tempted to take the money and spend it down when they change employers. They of course incur the 10% federal penalty for early withdrawals made before age 59 1/2, plus regular income tax. This double bite can consume nearly half of the return built up by the investments inside the 401(k). Instead, if you transfer the proceeds from your old employer's plan to your new employer's, they can go on growing without any interruption or depletion.

Practice asset allocation and stick with it. Your apportionment of your money among mutual funds, following the asset allocation models laid out in Chapter 5, should be no different when it comes to your 401(k). For example, when you are in your 20s,stash 80% of your money in stock funds, putting 10% into large-cap funds, 25% in mid-caps, 30% into international funds and 15% into small-caps. Then put the other 20% into bond funds, with 15% going to corporates and 5% to a convertible or high-yield bond fund. Then in the same way follow the models for your 30s, 40s and 50s. You may find that you can't follow our allocation models exactly inside your 401(k). For example, say your employer's plan does not offer any international fund. In that case, spread the 30% you would have devoted to an international fund evenly among the other stock fund choices.

Then, when you start building your independent portfolio outside your 401(k), you might start out buying an international fund and as that grows, rejigger the allocations inside your 401(k) to take the international fund into account. In other words, your allocation should be based on all your investments together, not just your 401(k) or your other portfolio. Remember that the virtues of asset allocation are compromised if you don't follow the models.

Be sensible about your company's stock. Many employers make their stock exceptionally attractive to employees, with the result that some 401(k) accounts become dangerously underdiversified because there is simply too much company stock there. One come-on is increasing the amount the company will put up in matching employee contributions—for example, throwing in a dollar for each employee dollar for the purchase of company stock vs. only 50 cents on the dollar for buying other investments. Some companies even launched their 401(k)s offering no choice but their own stock to put into the plan. But a healthy diversification is one reason why federal rules strongly encourage a real choice of five or more funds in a 401(k).

So how much of your company's stock should you be holding? Figure out where it would go if you were to put it into one of the stock funds in your 401(k). Would it be in the growth fund portfolio? Or equity income? Whatever it is, figure your company stock as part of that fund. So if you are supposed to have, say, 20% of your money in a large-cap fund and your 401(k) features an equity-income fund full of large caps, and you feel safe having 10% of your money invested in your company's stock, cut back your equity-income fund to 10% of the total too, so you still wind up with 20% in large caps.

Refigure your portfolio no more than twice a year. One of the most dangerous temptations for some employees is to call the 800 number of the institution that maintains the funds for your company's 401(k) and obsessively move your money around. Many plans permit participants to do this on a daily basis, and apparently the feeling of power it imparts can be intoxicating.

Here's a common scenario: The stock market moves dramatically. It doesn't matter in which direction, because we are not talking about rational behavior. If it moves down, excited investors will want to take advantage of the drop to switch their investments to riskier, more aggressive choices. This is actually a smart impulse in general, but it has to be harnessed to a disciplined plan of investing like asset allocation. Otherwise it is merely a hysterical flailing about. If stock prices accelerate upward, a lot of investors are consumed by an irresistible desire to get aboard. This is generally a destructive impulse and is the basis for what market experts describe as the speculative froth that characterizes a "toppy" market—that is, one that has risen to its peak and is poised for a collapse.

CHAPTER 8

GETTING THE RIGHT KIND OF HELP

THERE ARE SEVERAL KINDS OF FINANCIAL ADVISERS you can turn to—primarily financial planners, money managers, stockbrokers and insurance company salespeople. The trouble is that if you link up with the wrong one, you could be wandering into a nightmare far worse than anything you could concoct on your own. Archives of the Securities and Exchange Commission and the National Association of Securities Commissioners are awash in thousands upon thousands of stories relating how some financial planner or broker or insurance salesman put unwitting clients into devastatingly inappropriate investments in order to collect a high commission for himself. The other reason for horror tales is less sinister but still inexcusable: stupidity and/or inexperience.

This chapter will tell you what these pros can do for you and to you, and how to find the best and then use them to *your* best advantage.

Food for thought: As you read through this chapter, try to compare the services you will pay for if you use one of these pros with your ability to do it for yourself. There are two kinds of people in personal finance terms—those who can do it all alone and those who really need help. If you can go it alone, by all means do so. No hired hand will bring the care and insight to the this job that you can bring yourself. But if you truly see that you don't have the interest or talent for the job, then find a pro—and soon.

FINANCIAL PLANNERS

These are the generalists in the group. They are supposed to be trained to help you with your budgeting, investing, insurance, retirement planning and so on. Because of this, financial planners have not been strong as investment money managers. In fact many of them are so weak in their overall knowledge of personal finance that close observers of this burgeoning field believe that incompetence is a far greater problem than greed.

If this introduction to the financial planner sounds grim, don't be turned off. The hard part is finding a really good one. If you can, you will have a gem of great value. Here's how to go about it:

Draw up a list of candidates. This is not as easy at it looks. You want quality, not quantity here, which means identifying at least three, preferably four or five planners who come recommended by your lawyer, banker or accountant, or by friends or relatives who are satisfied clients of planners. Every candidate should have at least three years of experience in the field and sport the relevant certification: **Certified Financial Planner (CFP)** is awarded by the International Board of Standards and Practices for Certified Financial Planners in Denver. Candidates have to pass a battery of tough exams on all of the areas of personal finance. **Chartered Financial Consultant (ChFC)** is awarded by the American College in Bryn Mawr, Pa., also based on rigorous exams, often to insurance agents or people with an insurance background.

You may run into two other terms when shopping for a planner. These designations are fine when the planner is also a CFP or ChFC. Otherwise they suggest a pro who is highly focused only on investing or taxes. They are: **Chartered Financial Analyst (CFA)**, awarded by the Association for Investment Management and Research in Charlottesville, Va. These are often money managers. **Personal Financial Specialist (PFS)**, awarded by the American Institute of Certified Public Accountants in New York City. These are often CPAs or other tax specialists.

Interview each candidate in person. This session should be free. If a planner insists on charging for it, cross him or her off your list and move on. If you feel rushed or you get the feeling that this person is not easy to talk to or get comfortable with, you needn't end the session abruptly; but you should also consider hiring such a planner only if he or she gets A-plus marks on every other score. Here are the questions to ask on that initial interview.

How do you get paid? The planner should quickly reveal to you which of three categories he or she falls into: fee-only, fee-and-commission or commission-only planner. This is the basic division in the financial planning profession and no pro should be anything but totally honest and open about it. Then the planner should disclose exactly how he or she is compensated.

Fee-only planners are generally preferable because they receive no commissions for recommending financial products and so have no conflict of interest over those recommendations. You can buy an entire financial plan tailored to your needs for a fee of roughly $2,000 to $5,000. You can also pay a flat hourly fee, typically $100 or more per hour, for specific advice. The fee-only planner will usually recommend no-load mutual funds or life insurance. Some will actually manage portfolios of mutual funds for you, charging an annual fee of 1% or so of assets.

Fee-and-commission planners may receive flat fees of $600 or so for a plan plus 3% to 5% commissions on investments that they sell to you. While your out-of-pocket expenses may seem lower than with a fee-only planner, you may in fact wind up paying two or three times more to the fee-and-commission planner when commissions are added in.

Commission-only planners operate under a total conflict-of-interest cloud, since they receive all of their income from the 3% to 5% commissions they charge for investments you buy from them.

What kinds of financial planning do you do? More and more planners specialize in retirement planning. But others focus on taxes, college costs, or small businesses. Make sure your planner's specialty matches your needs.

Are you registered with the Securities and Exchange Commission and the securities department in your state? This is considered by some experts as the absolute minimum qualification to look for. In short, if the planner hasn't registered with the SEC and is dealing with investment products, he or she may be violating federal law. And most states require that planners register with the state securities department. So while such registrations do not in any way guarantee competence or honesty, they do show that the planner is willing to comply with the law.

Which financial products do you usually sell? The answer to this one can be a solid-brass tipoff. As we mentioned above, only fee-and-commission planners and commission-only planners actually sell products. Fee-only planners sell services. So it is important to gauge how greedy planners who take commissions might get. For instance, if the planner sells primarily mutual funds, municipal bonds, government securities and the like, that's a good sign. But if he or she is quick to sell you a lot of life insurance, and follows that up with unit trusts—all high-commission products—beware. One useful test: if a planner doesn't urge you to fully fund your employer's 401(k) and instead tries to sell you variable annuities, you can be sure he or she cares more about commissions than your welfare. Another test: Find out if the planner sells the mutual funds or insurance products of only his or her company. If so, you can be sure that there is no chance you will be offered the best choices.

Have you ever been disciplined by any federal or state agency or professional body or been involved in arbitration with any clients? No matter what the planner's answer is, you can verify it with the agency in question and back away if the record is bad.

Will you give me a copy of your ADV Form, Part II? This is the form the planner is supposed to file with the SEC and the state and to show prospective clients on request. It is a disclosure form that covers the planner's education, fees, business background, investment style and whether he or she has ever been in trouble with a court or regulatory body. The SEC requires this form only from registered investment advisers, so planners who specialize in accounting or insurance needn't file an ADV. But anyone aiming to retire young and rich and looking for an adviser will necessarily want one who works with investments. So get that ADV, Part II. It is the single most revealing document about any investment-oriented planner. So much so that many planners will balk at giving you one. Don't take no for an answer.

Will you give me the names of three people who have been your clients for at least two years? Experienced planners who are confident about their work should be happy to comply. All they have to do is to secure the permission of these clients for you to call them. When you do, simply ask them about their overall satisfaction with the planner's service, what level of returns they have been getting on their investments under the planner's guidance, and whether they plan to remain his or her clients. You might also ask if they know other clients and whether they too seem happy with the planner. You can even call these additional clients if you feel that any more probing is needed. In any case, never accept any excuse from a planner for not giving you some client names.

Will you let me look at some of the plans you have developed for people like me? You should be able to examine at least three full-scale plans to see if advice was geared to the needs of individual clients or whether it was mostly the same generalized boilerplate from one client to the other. Also ask for follow-up reports to find out how well the planner may have adjusted his or her advice to keep up with changes in the investment markets or in the client's situation.

Do a record check. After grilling your candidates and making a choice, there is one last chore you should do: Verify for yourself whether the planner has been the subject of any disciplinary actions. They are far from rare, so this exercise can be revealing and, of course, very important to you. First call the SEC (202-942-7040) plus the securities department in your state. (Look under the state Department of Commerce in your local phone book.) If the planner happens to be a member of the National Association of Securities Dealers (800-289-9999), find out if any actions have been taken by NASD against your prospective adviser. Some dirty tricks that turn up in these checks include churning accounts (too much buying and selling of investments to increase commissions) and having clients make out checks in his or her name instead of to the brokerage or fund family that is selling you the investment.

While all the questioning and checking may sound more like a grand jury probe than a search for a personal finance pro, you would feel otherwise if you could take a brief tour of the cases of fraud and incompetence that turn up each year. (For a rundown, see the section later in this chapter on brokers.) And remember that the right planner will likely be with you for many years to come, maybe even well into your retirment. He or she has to be worth the time, money and trust you will be handing over year after year. Otherwise, your planner could turn out to be your personal financial dream wrecker. Take no such chances with your future.

MONEY MANAGERS

These are the pros whose services used to be reserved for the rich. But that is not the case anymore. You can have your own personal money manager with a stake of as little as $50,000 or so. Your money manager puts together a portfolio of stocks and bonds for you with the promise that it will beat the market over time. The idea has grown so popular with middle-class investors that so-called managed accounts are attracting more than $5 billion a year.

But is a money manager a good idea for you? Follow the judgment of trusted experts and don't even consider going this route with a wad of less than $100,000. Otherwise transaction fees tend to be so expensive that you are better off with mutual funds.

Above $100,000, however, money managers have much to offer. Many of them actually deliver on their promise to earn higher-than-average returns. This, in fact, has been easier to do in recent years, when most mutual fund managers have tended to lag the averages. In addition, you enjoy much greater flexibility than with a mutual fund. For instance, you can ask your money manager to delay taking capital gains by selling winning stocks until next year instead of this year, deferring taxes on your profit. And while mutual funds are required under law to distribute a part of their capital gains each year, you can keep on racking up gains with stocks in your managed portfolio without paying any tax until the stock is sold.

You can also express your own values or style, for example, by requesting that your money manager not buy tobacco stocks or that he or she buy aggressive growth stocks or shares in a sector of the economy that you are particularly attracted to.

If having a money manager appeals to you, then you should go through a process of selection similar to the one laid out above for financial planners. This time you needn't be quite so rigorous because money managers focus on only one area of finance—investing—and have to rise or fall on their performance there. (Judging a generalist, which most financial planners tend to be, is far less cut-and-dried.) Here's how to go about it:

Avoid 3% fees. This is a simple way to steer clear of brokerage wrap accounts that are so expensive that even a money manager who performs well would have trouble making you an above-average return because of the fees. Typically, instead of the 1% or 2% a year that a money manager may charge, you get a prepackaged plan that wraps the money manager's services, brokerage fees and other charges into a single 3% fee. Typically you don't even get to talk to the money manager, but instead go through the broker or financial planner who sold you into the plan.

Go through a specialist unless you get a great referral. A few lucky people know someone—a friend or relative—who has used a money manager for years and has enjoyed high returns and genuine satisfaction. If you have such a contact, by all means use it. But if you don't, it's wise to get help from an independent specialist known as an investment management consultant. These are often stock brokers who find money managers for clients. In return, they receive the brokerage commissions that your money manager generates for your account.

Generally consultants refer you to small independent money managers who can give you individual attention. In addition, the brokers usually discount their commissions as much as 40% for money managers, so your total annual cost should not exceed 2% of the value of your portfolio. But many such money managers also charge 15% to 20% of the return they make on your money. For example, if you place $100,000 with a money manager who makes it grow to $125,000 in a year, you would pay him up to $5,000 in addition to commission costs. This may sound excessive, but many clients are happy to pay at this rate if their money manager pretty consistently whips the averages.

You can locate a talent scout in your area by calling the Institute for Investment Management Consultants (602-922-0090). This organization will recommend brokers with substantial work and educational experience. Any of these broker-consultants should have at least a dozen managers with different investing styles for you to choose from.

Monitor the records of at least three money managers. After the consultant makes recommendations, you have to make sure he or she is not simply handing you over to a money manager who shunts commissions his or her way. So check performance records back at least five years. Then check the manager's record with a benchmark that mirrors his or her style—like the Russell 2000 index for a manager who specializes in small-company stocks or the Russell Earnings-Growth Index for a manager who buys growth stocks. The broker recommending the manager can provide you with such performance comparison data. You'll be able to tell if you have the stomach to hang on for the ups and downs experienced by a more aggressive manager, or, conversely, whether a more conservative approach garners returns that are too tepid for your goals.

Make sure the manager is registered with the SEC. While this won't guarantee performance, it will mean that you can ask for the manager's ADV—the very revealing form we described to you above in the section on finding a financial planner. Remember, you get it all here—the manager's experience, style, fees and record of any disciplinary actions taken against him or her by any regulatory agency.

Keep track of your pro's performance. You ought to be receiving from the broker who found your manager for you a quarterly breakdown of stocks and bonds in your portfolio, all buys and sells during the period and a comparison of your holdings' performance with at least one index, like the S&P 500 or the Russell 2000.

The more aggressive the manager is, the more patient you need to be with fluctuations in returns. But just as there may be some heart-stopping downdrafts, there should also be lifts that outweigh the losses and sweep you ahead over time. So if your manager's returns lag not only the market but similar managers for a year or more, it's time to find out if his approach has changed or if he's not the stockpicker he once was. Your consultant should be willing to discuss your concern and, if needed, find you a new manager.

STOCKBROKERS AND OTHER SALES PEOPLE

If you ever consider using a stockbroker or a sales representative of an insurance or mutual fund company, chances are it is because one among these legions has called you on the phone and made a pitch. Our general advice to you is to give such cold calls the cold shoulder.

In such an instance, you don't end up buying something; it gets sold to you.

Such salespeople operate with an inherent conflict of interest. They are usually selling a product, whether it is a stock, bond, mutual fund or insurance policy, that they are being told to promote. Either it is a product of the company they work for or is being marketed by that company. As a result, there is not even a semblance of objectivity to the advice you will get from such professionals. They may even call themselves financial planners, financial analysts or even investment bankers. That ploy alone should tip you off that they are not levelling with you. They are sales people first, last and always.

So why tell you all this if the message is just: DON'T? Because the message is really: IF. If a stockbroker passes a few simple tests you can put to him or her, just as you might put a planner or money manager through the paces, you may have found another one of those rare jewels who will actually help you make a lot of money. The run-of-the-cold-call broker today is not for you. But here are the characteristics of those who might be:

- Brokers whose recommendations are based on research they do on the own, not just on the often stale research handed out by their brokerage's securities analysts. The best brokers have always been independent stock pickers first and team players for their brokerages second.
- Brokers who actually own the stocks that are on their buy lists. This generally follows the point above about brokers doing their own research. This kind of self-confidence will surely help yours in your broker.
- Brokers who won't bother you by trying to sell you the products of their brokerages, which are all too often heavily loaded with sales commissions and management fees. For instance, how can a broker justify asking a load of up to 8 1/ 2% for recommending a mutual fund that—surprise!-is part of his employer's stable of funds?

Aside from these points, your prospective broker should submit to some of the same battery of questions we laid out above for planners and money managers. In particular, make sure you get to talk to a few of his or her seasoned customers, get background information on education, experience and investing style. Get fee and commission policies spelled out in black and white. And always call that toll-free hot line operated by the NASD (800-289-9999).

As a parting slap in the face on this subject, here are some numbers to think about whenever you contemplate hiring a financial services pro of any kind to help you make money. The NASD regularly publishes statistics on the evildoers turned up by its hotline and other efforts to weed out unethical practices in the securities industry.

Since the '90s began, each year the NASD has received around 4,000 or more complaints. Each year it expels as many as 40 firms. Each year it bars as many as 490 individuals. Some of the stories behind the stats display incomprehensible outrages, like robbing elderly people of their means of support by pushing them into scary, but high-commission, investments. What's so alarming is not that such people exist, but that so many of them seem to gravitate to the money game.

CHAPTER 9

HOW TO HANDLE THE BIGGEST WAD YOU'LL EVER OWN

TALK ABOUT DEFINING MOMENTS. The day will come when you are confronted with one of the greatest single responsibilities of your life. You will be told by your employer just how much your retirement will be worth. There will be your 401(k) and other company savings plans, which will be available as a lump sum. And, if you're really lucky, there will be a standard pension, which traditionally is doled out in monthly checks until the end of your life. This is the annuity approach.

But more and more, particularly among larger companies, you are given the option of taking this pension as a lump sum too. So don't be surprised if you are suddenly expected to make some heavy decisions involving a stash amounting to $1 million or more. Will you be ready to do the smart thing? If not, you could be stumbling into the biggest fiasco in your life.

Here is the absolutely essential question that you need to have the right answer for when the time comes: *Should I take my pension as a lump sum or an annuity—that is, a check a month for life?*

Now let's see what's at stake and just how you should proceed:

LUMP SUM OR ANNUITY?

Think about it: you receive a huge wad of cash that must finance the rest of your—and maybe your spouse's—life and you alone are responsible for investing it all. If the very idea frightens you, that may be the most eloquent argument in favor of your choosing an annuity instead of a lump sum. Even if you know a fair amount about personal finance and have been a reasonably successful investor for years, being out there on your own is different when you don't have a regular job to fall back on. And if you feel trepidation now, isn't it likely that after you're retired and you have less to occupy your mind that you'll worry even more? Maybe not be able to sleep well some nights when the stock or bond market is misbehaving? And you might wonder how meticulous you will be, as you get on in years, in tending your portfolio. In short, the best thing about an annuity is peace of mind. Period.

The worst thing about an annuity is just as simply stated: it doesn't keep up with inflation. Even Social Security gives you a cost-of-living raise every year (unless, of course, the cost of living doesn't go up). And that's where the unquestioned charm of the lump sum comes in.

But before you make a lunge for a lump, a little examination of conscience is in order. Is it true that the very size of the sum makes you feel invincible? As if you could never run out of money with a cache that humongous? Or are you moved by the warming thought of living off the returns of your lump sum and then being able to leave most or even all if it to your children or grandchildren? If either of these emotions floods your being when you contemplate grabbing for a lump sum, you had better back off and think this thing through.

Yes, it's perfectly understandable that you'd be impressed with the size of a lump sum and yearning to pass it on to your progeny. But these emotions often make for poor logic and really rotten finance. They may mean that you are willing to fudge the one vital question within the lump-or-annuity question itself: *Will taking the lump sum serve your retirement finances better than taking the annuity?*

An obscure but important provision of a 1994 law requires employers to switch to what can be higher interest-rate and life-expectancy assumptions in computing their so-called defined benefit pensions that are distributed as lump sums. This can have the effect of significantly reducing the size of lump-sum payouts, particularly for employees who are now a number of years from retirement. The result, according to experts who have worked out the numbers, could reduce lump-sum pensions as much as 30% to 60% for many workers now in their 30s and 40s. Companies are free to make the switch in assumptions when they want, provided it is completed by the year 2000.

When your company's human resources people give you all the relevant numbers just before retirement, you will likely be asked to choose between a lump sum and several annuity alternatives. The single-life figure will be the highest, of course, since it covers only you. And you'll have to get your spouse to waive his or her rights to your pension if you decide to take the single-life option.

Then there's the joint-and-survivor annuity, which keeps on paying out to your spouse after you die, generally in amounts ranging from 50% to 100% of what you might have been getting. Of course, the more the survivor gets, the less your monthly check is going to be from the start.

Caveat: Insurance companies have a neat retirement-planning device that sounds a lot better than it is. The idea is to go ahead and take the single annuity and its larger monthly paycheck and to use part of the difference to buy a life insurance policy on your life, which protects your spouse. But experts largely disdain this approach, advising you to take the joint annuity. Not only is it safer, but a couple taking the life-insurance route runs the risk of not being able to afford maintaining coverage large enough to provide the income protection a spouse might need.

When trying to make up your mind, remember that your 401(k) will come to you in a lump sum. So if you choose to take your pension as an annuity, that can serve as the income portion of your portfolio, while the 401(k) lump becomes the growth and inflation-protection part.

So let's say you believe you are competent to handle your huge nestegg yourself, or perhaps you have an experienced and trustworthy adviser who can do it for you. In this case, you can confidently consider taking the lump. You can act to protect the value of the sum from inflation by investing it in growth-stock funds. You certainly can't do that with an annuity check. And besides, you can get at the principal anytime you need to if emergencies arise or if, say, you decide you have more than enough for yourself and want to start giving something to your heirs.

Here is a very rough rule of thumb you can use to give you an idea if the lump sum is a good deal: Ask your company's benefits department what the effective interest rate is on your pension when taken as an annuity. If the rate is lower than the rate of 30-year Treasury bonds, you would be better off taking the lump sum and buying Treasuries. But if the interest rate on the pension is higher than the Treasury bond rate, you would do well to take the annuity.

This is not to say you should rely solely on the rule of thumb when deciding between a lump sum and an annuity. In any case, it is imperative—repeat, *imperative*—that you get professional help at this time. An experienced tax accountant or retirement planner has the know-how and the software needed to run the numbers both ways and make the technical evaluations needed to come to an informed judgment.

For instance, do you seriously think you can competently crunch all these factors: an annuity income, its implied interest rate, inflation effects over 30 or so years; and on the other hand a lump sum amount with its implied interest rate and a reasonable return on that money; *plus* how well both alternatives fit with the rest of your assets? You would have to be familiar with complicated actuarial assumptions and truly mind-numbing tax rules.

ROLLOVER IRA OR AVERAGING?

If you decide to go for the lump, you're immediately catapulted into another either/or decision. Sorry about that. But this one makes a huge difference in how your money will be taxed. You can choose to take the money and pay tax on it right away, using a highly favorable tax-cutting scheme called special averaging. Or you can roll the money over into an IRA and avoid tax on it until you begin taking it out. Both ways have advantages and disadvantages, which we will cover below.

Warning: The law is draconian on exactly how you handle the money at the time it is paid out: If you go the IRA route but fail to roll over your money into an IRA within 60 days of receiving it, you are immediately liable to payment of taxes on it. And you have to be extra careful in how the rollover is made. As strong as the impulse may be to hold that much in your hands just for an hour or so, resist it. Instead, you should let your company perform the rollover to the brokerage house, mutual fund company, bank or insurance company of your choice. Otherwise your employer will have to withhold 20% of the wad before handing it over to you. That 20% comes back to you only after you claim a credit for it on your next annual tax return. And that's a hassle and a half.

Now let's take a look at the two methods and then evaluate them.

Five- or 10-year averaging allows you to figure your tax as if you had received your lump sum over a five- or 10-year period. Spreading out the amount in this fashion drops you into lower brackets than you otherwise would have to face. Unfortunately, five-year averaging is under a death sentence: it will disappear in the year 2000. If you're retiring before then, you are one of the lucky ones who can consider this generous loophole. As for 10-year averaging, only those born before 1936 are allowed to use it.

In addition, to gain entry into the averaging enclosure, your lump sum distribution must pass all of the following four tests:

First, it must be from a qualified pension, profit-sharing, stock-bonus or Keogh plan you participated in for at least five years. Ask your plan administrator at work if your company's plan qualifies.

Second, it must consist of the entire balance due you from all of your employer's plans.

Third, It must be paid to you within a single tax year. Say you retire in March and pay your taxes on a calendar-year basis: then you must receive your entire balance by December 31 of that year.

Fourth, it must be paid after you turn 59 1/2. (If you were born before January 1, 1936, however, this rule does not apply.)

If you square with these requirements, you can apply averaging to the taxable portion of your lump sum: Your own nondeductible contributions are not taxable since they were made with your own after-tax dollars; but all your employer's contributions to your account plus its earnings through the years are taxable to you. Your employer will issue to you a Form 1099-R, and you will find the taxable amount listed there.

You might want your accountant to figure your tax if you use averaging, but it isn't at all complicated if you want to have a go at it yourself. First you divide the amount by five or 10 (see below for the difference). For instance, say your lump sum amounts to $200,000 not counting any nondeductible contributions of yours. In this case, the whole $200,000 is taxable. With five-year averaging, one-fifth of the total is $40,000. Then you find the tax on that amount, using the rates for single taxpayers. (These are listed in the IRS instruction booklet for filing your annual tax return.) You will probably wind up saving as much as half the tax you otherwise would have to pay without averaging.

You figure 10-year averaging the same way you would five-year averaging except that you divide and multiply by 10 instead of five. One major difference: If you use the 10-year method, you will have to use the higher and more steeply graduated 1986 tax rates for singles, which range from 11% to as high as 50%. Current rates run from 15% to 39.6%. In case you qualify for both five-and 10-year averaging, get IRS Form 4972, which you can use to compute your tax both ways and find out which one will save you more.

Rollovers

IRA rollovers permit you to postpone paying any tax on your lump sum until you withdraw it. You can put your money into one, two, or more IRAs, as you like. And if you also have a Keogh plan, which you would have set up with earnings from self-employment, you can do a rollover plus reserve your right to five- or l0-year aveaging too. Here's how you do it: Put your lump-sum distribution into the Keogh; later on, you can take a lump-sum distribution from it and use averaging to compute your tax.

Doing a rollover is simple; you just have to make sure it's done correctly. Have your employer transfer the money directly to your IRA or IRAs. This avoids having 20% of the payout withheld. And if you're under 59 1/2, you also avoid being nicked for an unrefundable 10% early-withdrawal penalty on the 20% unless you make it up out of your own pocket. You cannot include your own after-tax contributions to the plan or any lump-sum severance pay in the rollover. If you do, you will get hit with a 6% excise tax on the excess amount.

If you don't want to roll over your total distribution, you can take part of it yourself and pay regular income tax on it (plus the 10% early-withdrawal penalty if you're under 59 1/2). But if you make such a split, you can't use averaging. You are required to report a rollover on line 16 of your 1040 for that year. If you omit this information, the IRS will figure you are not reporting regular income and will send you a hefty tax bill.

And the choice is...the IRA, usually. Consider this example: a $250,000 distribution was made in 1994 to a 62-year-old retiree in the combined 34% federal and state tax bracket. An annual before-tax return of 6.5% is expected. Ten years later, when the retiree is 72, here are the results. If a rollover IRA had been chosen for the $250,000, no immediate tax would be paid and the accumulated assets by age 72 would be $440,643. With 10-year averaging, $44,118 would be immediately taken away in tax, leaving only $205,882 available for investment. The upshot in 10 years: accumulated assets totaling $300,471.

With five-year averaging, $55,635 would be taxed right away, with only $194,365 available for investment. After 10 years, the accumulated assets would amount to $283,663. The IRA rollover wins by a country mile. Of course, when the retiree started withdrawing the money, he or she would have to pay taxes at the regular income tax rate, which could be higher later on. It almost surely would be higher than the reduced rate under averaging.

The wisest thing to do before settling on a rollover would be to ask your accountant or financial planner to figure the current tax on your lump sum using five-year averaging and 10-year averaging too if you qualify. Also have the tax pro make an estimate of the tax you would pay on future distributions from an IRA. Then compare the two, making sure that the pro accounts for the return you will make on the IRA.

Even if the IRA wins out on all counts, there are times when people need large amounts of cash right away. For instance, you may want to start a new business. Then by all means use the averaging method. Even though it may not save you as much in taxes as an IRA, it is a prudent compromise.

CHAPTER 10

FIVE YEARS TO GO: WHAT TO DO

THE AGE YOU HAVE ALWAYS WANTED TO RETIRE IS, unbelievably, only five years away. No matter how carefully you have been planning your retirement finances through the years, you should stop now and review some of the factors that will make or break that dream. Five years isn't much time if you're just beginning to save. But it is just about right for a close look followed by a careful repositioning of your finances. That way there will be no hair-raising surprises during the months leading up to your retirement date. (Your failsafe mechanism: Chapter 11, coming up next, which offers a last-minute checklist.) Take the following 10 points to heart and you won't become a pre-retirement head case:

1. REFIGURE HOW MUCH YOU'LL NEED

This is point number one for a very good reason. Just as completing the worksheet in Chapter 3 was an absolute, no-question-about-it necessity, going back and re-doing that worksheet is now just as critical. This exercise will tell you just how wide you are of the mark.

What if it turns out after re-completing the worksheet that you are seriously short of the total capital you will need to accumulate before you retire? Then the very next move you make is to . . .

2. RECONCILE YOUR PLAN TO REALITY

If your shortfall is major, and you are sure you have been religiously following a plan, then you should first find out what went wrong with your plan. Did your income fail to keep up with expectations? Did your choice of mutual funds underperform? While it is a little late to be finding out such things, they happen. More likely, though, you will find yourself short by a non-catastrophic amount that you might even be able to make up over the next five years. There are several routes you can take, singly or in combination:

First, increase your savings. Can you turn around and save like mad for five years? If so, do it. If you haven't been saving all your raises and bonuses, start there. If you are in the neighborhood of 50, be aware that you are at a dangerous age as a consumer. You're at your earning peak and the two central spending drains of your life—the house and the kids—are at last off your back. So bit by bit and oh so imperceptibly, you and your spouse have begun treating yourselves to better (and longer) vacations, a nicer wardrobe, a jazzier car (or two) and a couple of mellow restaurant dinners a week. You know where the fat is. Tell yourself it's only for five years, and cut, cut, cut. And invest it all.

Second, put off your retirement date. As mentioned earlier, accruals in your company benefits often accelerate as you get closer to retirement. This is particularly true with old-fashioned defined-benefit pensions. Also, your 401(k) continues to grow, spurred by your employer's contributions and profit sharing. Do a back-of-the-envelope calculation to see roughly how much each year of work adds to your nestegg and then decide whether it is worth it to hang in there for a year or two more.

Third, invest more aggressively. This of course means increasing your risk close to retirement. This is not always the right thing to do and if done without care, it could be a major mistake. It would be very easy in today's volatile markets, for instance, to move money to riskier investments when they are relatively expensive and then have to sell them when they are down. But sometimes taking on extra risk could be the right thing to do, particularly if you haven't followed the asset allocation set out in Chapter 5 and your portfolio is too conservative in the first place. Among the signs: less than half of your investments are in stocks or stock mutual funds; your stock funds are all low-risk equity-income types, and you are shy on growth and aggressive growth funds; more than a quarter or so of your money is in cash-equivalent funds like those that hold GICs. If you're thinking of getting more aggressive, you may want to do it with professional help.

3. CONSIDER HIRING A PRO

You may have gotten this far on your own, and that may be fine. If you know that your savings and investments are keeping pace with the timetable you set up for yourself, no crisis looms on the horizon, and you have been a careful student of your personal finances all through the years, there may be no need to think about getting professional help.

On the other hand, if you are falling behind in your nestegg accumulation, your investment picks are not performing well, or you have other questions you don't feel competent to handle yourself, it may be time to look for a *really good* financial planner. If you wonder why the emphasis is on the *really good*, a quick review of Chapter 8, Getting the Right Kind of Help, will refresh your memory.

A fee-only planner who comes highly recommended is usually your best bet, particularly at a time when you have a considerable portfolio of investments. The temptation for a commission planner to dump those investments in favor of ones that will bring him or her commissions might be too great to fight. And the itch to sell you financial products you don't need, like costly life insurance, annuities or long-term-care insurance, might be equally irresistible.

When you find a planner you like, make sure you are completely comfortable with—and totally understand—every move he or she recommends. For example, if the planner wants you to pay, say, $2,000 for a full financial plan, make him or her explain what benefit someone five years from retirement would get from it. (Little, unless it's a post-retirement plan, and now might be a little soon for that.)

4. START PAYING OFF ALL YOUR PERSONAL DEBT

It is generally a healthy idea to enter retirement debt-free. After all, you will almost certainly be living on a smaller income than your present one, and you will want to leave as much as you can to grow in your investment portfolio instead of using it for expenses. The only exception to this rule has to do with your house. If, for instance, you are still carrying a substantial mortgage, and current mortgage rates are two points or so below the rate you are carrying, you may want to look into refinancing. If you wait until after you retire, banks may be less eager to do business with you when you are no longer receiving a full salary. Also check out the cost of shortening the term of the mortgage, which will save you lots of interest dollars in the long run. And consider a fixed instead of an adjustable mortgage. As a general rule, it is prudent to keep as many as possible of your post-retirement expenses fixed.

5. FOCUS HARDER ON WHERE YOU WILL LIVE

Granted, there's a huge emotional element in this decision. Perhaps that's why most retirees just stay put in the home they've lived in for many years. But more and more people are investigating the adventuresome option of retiring in a different part of the country or of the world. The reason we bring this up now is that there is also a huge financial element involved as well. So the earlier you decide on where and when, the better. Here are some leading considerations if:

You stay put. Will you be able to pay off your mortgage by the time you retire? If not, how long will you have to deal with this major expense? Have you considered the possibility of moving to a smaller place in your town or neighborhood? That way you would be staying put in your community but possibly sharply reducing your carrying charges, property taxes and energy bills while at the same time pocketing the difference between what you got for your old larger house and what you pay for the new one.

You trade down. Typically, those people who retire and move south—to Florida, for instance—wind up with a windfall like the one we just described: the difference between what their new house costs and what they got for their old one.

If this is your plan, even though it's five years early, you should estimate how much that wad will amount to and figure it into your post-retirement finances. It could make a big difference, and even inspire you to retire earlier than you thought you could. Another key point: If you are planning to move to a distant place, it is essential to spend as much time there in as many seasons of the year as you can before you make a final decision. Five years before R Day is not too soon to start these pilgrimages.

You buy a second home. This is the choice of many retirees who want to hold onto the homestead and have a retreat in the sun or up at the lake. While this is of course the most expensive way to go, many retirees do it with an eye to eventually giving up the homestead and making the vacation house their full-time retirement home.

Whatever your decision, it will involve considerable variations in costs. You should work these out, at least in the rough, so you will be sure you can afford the expenses. Doing the math may also cause you to alter your plans. If so, you shouldn't wait until you're on the brink of retirement before finding out the financial facts.

6. TAKE A WHOLE NEW LOOK AT YOUR ASSET ALLOCATION

Way back in Chapter 5, you learned that an amazing 92% of an investor's returns come from the correct combination of assets. You also read that study after study confirmed that investors are generally too conservative with their money, with the result that their portfolios don't grow as fast as they otherwise would. And even in this chapter, you were invited—very carefully—to consider getting more aggressive in your investments if you found yourself falling behind in your capital accumulation plan. Now, after all that, you're being asked to take a completely fresh, objective look at your asset allocation. What gives? Doesn't anybody trust you? Well, yes and no. This matter transcends trust. It is just that important.

What you should do is simple:

First, put together all of your investments, those inside your 401(k) or other tax-deferred plan, any other company savings plan, annuities, Keoghs, IRAs, and any bank and brokerage accounts you have. Leave nothing out. When you allocate, you have to do it with all of your assets.

Second, go back to your basic allocations (Chapter 5 again) for each age and see how your current allocation veers from your original plan.

Third, rejigger by reducing and adding to the amounts you have in various mutual funds until your overall portfolio is back in line with your allocation model.

That's all. Sounds almost too simple, but you might be amazed at how far a set of investments can drift off their allocated course.

Oh, one more thing. Don't forget to do this every year from now on.

7. CHECK YOUR LIFE INSURANCE

If you're like most people, you have never developed the habit of pulling your life insurance policies out of the drawer and evaluating them every few years. Chances are the only time you pay close attention to them is when an insurance salesman comes calling, and you soon find yourself the owner of a brand new policy.

The point here is that your greatest need for life insurance may have passed, yet you may be paying high premiums that are being at least partly wasted. So gather up your policies. Look over your responsibilities. Are your offspring grown and out of the house? Are you not the sole breadwinner? If you were to die, would your spouse and other dependents be financially secure *without* the proceeds of your insurance? If so, you are overinsured.

You may still want to carry some coverage, but should it be in cheaper term life or in more expensive whole life, with its cash buildup? Do you know whether your employer will continue to insure you after you retire? If you've found a reliable fee-only financial planner, he or she can help you sort your life insurance questions out. Or you can call an outfit like the Life Insurance Advisers Association (800-521-4578). For a fee, an adviser will assess your coverage and costs for you.

8. MAKE REALISTIC PLANS ABOUT POST-WORK WORK

You can look on this as one of your escape valves. By working out an honest assessment of your employment possibilities after retirement, you accomplish two wonderfully confidence-building things. First, you identify another income source should you need it. Second, you create a potential outlet if you find that you don't want to live with retirement without some work.

And note the emphasis on realistic plans. Is there anyone who doesn't spend their working lives daydreaming about some ideal way of earning a living? Like running a great little restaurant or bed-and-breakfast or country hotel or bookstore antique shop? These enterprises are realistic for only a few people who have an entrepreneur's spirit and endless amounts of energy to expend on the long hours and, often, hard work. And everywhere you turn today, there are so many kinds of competition for small business that serenity is one thing you aren't likely to achieve on your own.

Again realistically, the opportunities for part-time or even full-time work for older people are in a state of renaissance. And that trend is sure to continue and expand just because it will be so hard for most people to retire and finance 30 years of retirement without continuing to work. Some experts believe, in fact, that the era of total retirement at 55 or 60 or 65 is already fading.

So your first homework assignment on the subject of working after retirement is to make a list of the kinds of work you're both good at and enjoy. Then start assessing the demand out there for what you have to supply. Keep on probing from time to time over the next four years. By your last pre-retirement year, you ought to have a short list of job prospects ready to pursue if and when you want to do so.

9. VISIT YOUR BENEFITS PEOPLE

It's a mistake to wait until near the very end to talk to your company's benefits department, because it is almost certain that there are topics that will substantially affect your retirement finances that you don't know enough about. Like:

Your pension. Now it the time to ask for an assessment of the size of your pension. It's essential that you know these numbers early so you can calculate your retirement finances in a more and more detailed way as you approach the jumping-off point. You'll most likely get an estimate of your annual pension, calculated in several ways: as a single-life annuity, as a 50% joint-and-survivor annuity, as a 100% joint-and-survivor annuity, as a 10-year period-certain annuity, and perhaps a couple of other ways.

The single-life amount will be the highest because it goes to you for the rest of your life. Period. The 10-year certain annuity will probably generate the next highest annual amount because it will be paid out for only 10 years if you should die earlier. Consequently, a 15-year-certain annuity pays a bit less. The 50% joint-and-survivor annuity comes next: it continues paying, say, your spouse half what you were getting should you die. A 100% joint-and-survivor, which keeps on paying the whole amount to your survivor, pays out the least from the start. And you will also receive an estimate of the amount of your lump sum if your employer allows you that choice.

Your medical benefits. These are changing more rapidly than in years as employers try to reduce the frightening growth of health-care insurance. Find out exactly how much your coverage will cost you after you retire. If you are retiring before 65, you'll have to wait until that age to get Medicare. Will the company help you out? And will it do anything for you after you turn 65? Like providing inexpensive medigap coverage as some generous employers do; or even long-term-care insurance, a small but fast-growing trend.

Your life insurance. Some employers maintain your coverage up to 65 even if you retire early. Some have other goodies that could enable you to cut way back on your private coverage.

Your spouse. Find out if your employer's post-retirement benefits are a lot better than those of your spouse's employer. You may want to enroll your spouse in your plan before you retire so that he or she will be able to share in those gifts after you both are retired.

Help. Ask what kind of guidance the company will give you as you prepare to retire. For instance, it may sponsor free seminars for you and your spouse held by knowledgeable pros. Make sure you sign up.

10. CALL SOCIAL SECURITY

You were supposed to do this when you filled in the worksheet in Chapter 3, Figuring Out How Much You Will Need. Since now is the right time to review everything, it would be wise to make that call again (800-772-1213) and get a completely up-to-date projection of your Social Security benefit.

CHAPTER 11

SIX MONTHS TO GO: WHAT TO DO

GLORY BE, THE END IS NEAR. But first there are a few things you'll need to act on during the final six months before your last 'night, all. Do each of them carefully and with deliberate speed. The old warning about hasty marriages serves well here too: Retire in haste, repent at leisure. Thirty years' worth.

1. RE-REFIGURE HOW MUCH YOU'LL NEED

In Chapter 10 you were advised to refigure the worksheet in Chapter 3 that shows you how much you need to save each year so you'll have enough for your retirement. Now is the moment in your life when you get to tot up all the saving and investing you've done over the years to see how close you are to what you'll need.

If you carefully followed the advice in Chapter 10, you won't get any nasty surprises now. But you should at least review the worksheet this one last time because all of the figures you've entered on it—which are just rough estimates when you're decades away from retirement—will be at their firmest now. So you'll get the most credible bottom line now. If by some chance you are wide of the mark, review Chapter 10 for advice on what to do about it. If, for instance, it is too late to put off your retirement, you're saving all you can and you don't dare get more aggressive in your investing, you may need to look into post-retirement employment.

2. NOTIFY YOUR COMPANY'S BENEFITS DEPARTMENT

The folks who process your retirement paperwork—human resources, benefits, personnel or whatever they're called at your company—usually want you to tell them your planned retirement date about six months ahead. While this is convenient for them, it is also helpful for you because you will be going over a number of complicated issues that you will want to think about, then go back with any questions you may have. For instance, the benefits people will be computing the final numbers for your pension and they will be explaining what benefits you will lose, which ones will be cut back and which ones, if any, will stay in place. The next two points expand on these matters.

3. REWIRE YOUR BENEFITS

As indicated in Chapter 10, the principal ones you'll be looking at are health and life insurance. Since Medicare won't kick in until you're 65, early retirement may mean footing the entire bill for your health-care coverage until then. Your benefits people may be able to help you here. Your group life insurance will likely end when you retire, or possibly stay in force until you're 65. In either case, you may not need the kind of death-benefit coverage you had to have when you had small children. You may not need any life insurance at all for that matter. Many retirees have policies solely for use in helping settle their estates. But that's an entirely different matter that must be discussed with your financial planner or an estate lawyer. Your company disability insurance may also have outlived its usefulness, unless you are sure you will need to work to some extent after you retire.

4. DECIDE: LUMP SUM OR ANNUITY

Remember from Chapter 9: annuities can't keep up with inflation, but if you manage a lump sum well you can invest for growth and thereby conquer that rapacious inflation beast. The catch: you have to manage it well, and that's a big responsibility. Well, now comes the moment of truth. You must choose between the two, and your decision will be irrevocable.

A smart, honest fee-only financial planner can be of great help in making up your mind. He or she will not only assess your strengths and weaknesses as a money manager, but can also analyze the annuity and the lump sum and tell you if one or the other is a better deal. The analysis is complex: don't think about doing it yourself and don't leave it in the hands of a planner you don't trust.

5. WORK OUT WHERE YOUR STASH WILL BE INVESTED

If you take an annuity, you don't have to worry about this point as far as your pension is concerned. If you take a lump sum, you have to determine the disposition of it *plus* your 401(k) or other tax-favored savings plan. Assuming you roll the money over into an IRA, usually the best deal, you must tell your company where to direct the funds, and it all must be done within 60 days. This will probably mean choosing a mutual fund family or families.

Your financial planner will guide you on this move. If you don't have a planner you must do your homework during this period.You not only need to become familiar with fund families, but choose which funds within your chosen family you want to put your money into. Use the asset allocation outlined for your age in Chapter 5. And if you haven't done so already, start reading newspapers and magazines, such as MONEY, that feature strong mutual fund coverage.

6. SET UP A HOME-EQUITY LINE OF CREDIT

If you've followed the advice in Chapter 10, you will by now have paid off your personal debt, or at least most of it. Even though your credit record may be exemplary, lenders may become a lot less eager to let you borrow once you are retired and your income has shrunk. So just in case an emergency surfaces and you really need to borrow, set up a home-equity line of credit now. You can draw on it any time you want and take out as much as you want without having to go through the standard credit routine. The interest is not only far lower than that on credit cards, but it is also fully deductible. Since making use of this credit line puts your home in hock, use it sparingly. Another reasonable use: to consolidate your debts and reduce their cost.

7. CHECK OUT REVERSE-MORTGAGE DEALS

These provide you with a way to give yourself a second pension tied to the value of your house. You gradually sell the equity in your home to a bank, getting monthly checks in a kind of reversal of the standard mortgage, which requires you to send the bank a monthly check. These can be lifesavers for retirees who see they are running out of money.

Here's another way of looking at the reverse mortgage if you're determined to retire early but find six months ahead of the target date that the numbers just don't add up, that you will need more than you have to finance that 30-year golden phase. You may want to use some of your retirement plan money to open a business; the income from a reverse mortgage could take the place of that cash.

But what of the risk? Is it prudent to gamble with the roof over your aging head? You can avoid that danger by taking out a *tenure reverse mortgage*, which brings you those monthly checks for the rest of your life. The alternative is the *term reverse mortgage*, which runs for a set time, usually no more than 20 years. Then the bank sells the house. The older you are, the more you get in your checks. A single person with a house worth $200,000 might receive around $700 a month at age 70, running up to $1,500 a month at age 85. Generally to qualify for a reverse mortgage, one of the spouses must be at least 62 and the mortgage must be paid off.

8. DECIDE ABOUT SOCIAL SECURITY

If you are at least 62 when you retire, you can start receiving your Social Security checks right away. But you should apply for them a few months before they're supposed to start so you won't miss any. But remember that if you do start on Social Security at 62, you will get only 80% of the total benefit for the rest of your life. It's a complicated decision, and one you need to make in the context of your entire financial outlook. For instance, it might be better to jump in at 62 if it means being able to leave your retirement money growing undisturbed in your rollover IRA for a longer time.

9. START LETTING GO

Now, during these last six months, is the time to start distancing yourself from the world of your office. You don't have to start finding fault with your boss or your colleagues. Far from it. The trick is to focus your thoughts more and more on what you will be doing after you call it quits. What will the days be like? Have you thought about how you'll structure them? What will your first project be? Your second? You mean you haven't yet started planning the most dreamed-about trip of your life? There's so much to do, so much to think about. There. You're letting go already. It's all right to look back, but not for too long.